organizing for life

organizing for life

declutter your mind to declutter your world

sandra felton

Revell

Grand Rapids, Michigan

© 1989, 2002, 2007 by Sandra Felton

Published by Fleming H. Revell
a division of Baker Publishing Group
P.O. Box 6287, Grand Rapids, MI 49516-6287
www.revellbooks.com

New paperback edition published 2007

Previously published under the title *Messie No More*

Printed in the United States of America

Library of Congress Cataloging-in-Publication Data
Felton, Sandra.
    Organizing for life : declutter your mind to declutter your world / Sandra
Felton.
        p.   cm.
    ISBN 10: 0-8007-3185-9 (pbk.)
    ISBN 978-0-8007-3185-4 (pbk.)
    1. House cleaning. I. Title.
TX324.F4433 2007
648'.5—dc22   2006025454

Because we are made in God's image we desperately want to look at our own creation and say that it is good. Are the following lies keeping you from creating a beautiful and orderly home?

Lie: Being messy is a superior way of life.
Truth: When the house is messy and our lives are disorganized, we lose touch with what is peaceful and noble in ourselves, and our self-image suffers.

Lie: Messies need more willpower and discipline.
Truth: Messies need focus, not fogginess.

Lie: Working harder will keep your house clean.
Truth: You already work hard enough! You have to uncover the underlying causes.

Lie: I'm a hopeless Messie.
Truth: Getting a house under control requires nothing that we do not have or cannot get. You have an orderly person within you.

Let these and countless other truths transform you into a Messie no more!

By Sandra Felton

contents

acknowledgments

I would be remiss if I did not mention the help I received from the teachers and librarians at Hialeah High School. These learned women lay me in the shade in many ways. Any references I have needed and leads I have asked for they have given me. Through their conversations in the faculty lounge and the library, they have unknowingly been my advisors.

I value the inspiration and information I receive from people attending my seminars and workshops and from others I meet. Many offer perceptive comments and exhibit courage that is invaluable to me in sharpening my understanding of the importance of organization in women's lives. From them I have gained a better understanding of the need to live with dignity and effectiveness and to use our qualities to the fullest extent.

Special thanks to Bob Schwartz who wrote *Diets Don't Work*. His understanding of the search for normalcy in the area of weight control has been a great help to me in understanding my search for normalcy in the area of order in the home. He and I met once as guests on a television show, and if I had known then what I know now about his book, I would have thanked him in person—many times.

don't skip this introduction

Nothing is more frustrating than being required to do something beyond our ability. Those of us who call ourselves Messies live daily with the reality of this problem. We want to keep the house in order and beautiful, but many of us find it next to impossible to do so.

There are many examples of this kind of problem, but perhaps none illustrates the situation better than the story of Rumpelstiltskin.

The miller in the story had a clever daughter, and he boasted to the king that she could spin straw into gold. The king loved gold, so he locked the girl into a room filled with straw and ordered her to perform her miracle.

Rumpelstiltskin learned that the beautiful miller's daughter had been asked to do the impossible, and he took advantage of the situation. Appearing miraculously through the locked door, he promised to spin the straw into gold if the girl would give him her ring. She agreed, knowing it was the only way she could save her life.

But the king was not satisfied with one roomful of gold. He brought in another load of straw for the miller's daughter to transform. Again Rumpelstiltskin appeared, this time demanding the girl's necklace as payment.

Still not satisfied, the king commanded the young girl to work her magic for a third time. Rumpelstiltskin appeared again, but this time he demanded the girl's firstborn son.

Messies can sympathize with the miller's poor daughter. Many Messies are bright and creative. Because of this, people expect them to be able to perform simple housekeeping chores without any problem. We expect it of ourselves. But it seems as impossible for us as it was for the miller's daughter to spin straw into gold. Neither threats nor promises move us toward success. We wish for a little elf to come in and do the job for us, but he never arrives.

This book is the next best thing. It won't clean your house for you, and it doesn't come with coupons for maid service, but it will help you develop the mind-set that makes messiness a thing of the past.

Many who read this book are desperate to change and don't know how. Many have tried various methods and slipped back into old habits. Some keep things picked up but at the price of great physical and emotional effort. They have improved but find it hard to keep it up. Many of these strugglers feel very much alone. Quietly, doggedly, daily, they fight the clutter, which, like the tide, is constantly coming in. Their husbands may be urging them to do better. Their children may be embarrassed. They may feel like failures because they can't get things moving in the right direction. Whether their house is terribly messy or just consistently more cluttered than they want it to be, they feel it is out of control no matter how hard they work to control it.

Most of us already know how to do more than we are doing, so this is not another "how to" book. It does, however, contain many practical ideas geared for Messies. It has some information your mother never told you (or she told you when you weren't listening). All of it will help you move toward the goal of order and beauty in your life. But it only works when you are mentally and emotionally ready to work at it.

This book is a "why" book. It clarifies for many of us what is at the root of our messiness. A friend showed me weeds from her yard. She was so amazed at how long the roots were that she taped them to a paper and recorded the measurement of the top of the weed in relation to the root. The result was startling. One weed had a tiny little top, maybe a half inch tall. But the root! That root went on for three and a half inches! To keep the weeds out of her life permanently, she had to dig deep and remove it all.

So it is with some of us concerning the issue of disorganization in our lives. Sometimes the messes keep coming back because we haven't given enough attention to removing the roots. I hope this book will help you with that.

Like many books, this book tells us what we may already know but don't know that we know.

In this book you will discover the reasons your house is out of control. Then you will learn ways to get things back under control and keep them that way. I know it sounds too good to be true, but it's not. Your friends and neighbors who are not neat freaks don't have cluttered houses, do they? They don't even seem to be interested in housekeeping. How do they do it? What is their secret? You're about to find out.

This book contains the basis for a permanent change. In its own way, it is the foundational book of the Messies Anonymous program. It requires some written participation that is essential for accomplishing your purposes. Your written responses are an important part of the changes you will make.

If you don't want anyone to know what you are reading, cover the outside and write "The Total Watercress Health Diet" or some such inane thing across the front. That should keep folks out.

This book is one of several I have written on the topic of messiness. Others include *The Messies Manual, When You Live with a Messie,* and *Organizing Magic.* Each has a place in bringing the message of hope to Messies who feel hopeless.

A disclaimer is in order here. This book is not written so you can give a name to your problem and thereby give the problem an excuse for being. It is written to open the door for appropriate solutions to your problems. I am a professional organizer with a master's degree in education, but my main qualification is that I am just one poor beggar telling others where I have found bread. It is up to you to follow through and get the bread. Each problem is accompanied by possible solutions, suggested books, and places to find more help.

One more disclaimer is in order. I am an eclectic reader, so I draw material from many—sometimes unlikely—sources. Like a butterfly sipping from one blossom and then another, I do not check the type of soil each flower is growing in. In other words, when I refer to an idea or quote an author I am not necessarily endorsing the overall philosophy. I leave it to the readers' good judgment to discern those things for themselves.

it's not about the house

It's not about the house. It really isn't. It's about the person who lives in the house, and that's you.

You may go to your neighbors' houses, as I did, and find them sipping coffee at ten in the morning, surrounded by tidy areas and shining surfaces. You, on the other hand, don't want to invite others to your place. If you are like I was, you may not even want to spend much time there yourself. Too much disorder, clutter, and mess. That translates into frustration, emotional drain, and just plain work for you—when you do it.

I used to dream of moving into a new apartment, leaving all of my things (and maybe even my family) behind, and starting over clean. My longing was palpable. I yearned for order, beauty, harmony, peace—anything to get the burden of messiness off my back.

Rhett Butler expressed my sentiments exactly as he walked away from his chaotic life with Scarlett O'Hara: "I want peace. I want to see if somewhere there isn't something left in life of charm and grace." But charm and grace sure weren't in my house. And I didn't have anywhere else to go except back to my daily struggle with clutter.

Deep down I knew it wasn't about the house. If my imaginary apartment had become real, it would have become just as cluttered, with or without my family, as the house I wanted to leave behind.

It was about me. I was the one constant that made every place I lived the same. I was doing something, something mysterious that I was unaware of, that invariably muddled my environment wherever I went. What was it?

As it turned out, there were several things—things that are addressed in this book. Things that are at work in your life, as they were in mine, without your knowledge. The proof of their existence is evident as you look around you. Chapter by chapter in this book, they are spotlighted for you to examine and, if necessary, to challenge.

Thousands of people from all around the world, mostly but not always women, have been asking themselves the same questions I asked myself. Through other books I have written, through the website www.messies.com, through both local and online groups, the message has spread. As the concepts I learned and taught have jumped from country to country and culture to culture, we have seen that the problem of disorganization and its ramifications in life are amazingly similar everywhere.

Some people seek help through the books that have been translated into German, Dutch, and Spanish. Chinese and Portuguese publishers have also inquired about translations. English editions are in the United States, Australia, South Africa, Great Britain, and other countries where English is read. Some people come through www.messies.com and the online support groups that join people all over the world in a unified quest for order. Still others are drawn to help through local Messies Anonymous groups. Disorganized strugglers are definitely not alone. Messiness has proven to be an equal opportunity problem and does not observe race, creed, or national origin, as the saying goes.

For us all, no matter our location or circumstance, the house first starts to change in the heart and mind. Buy into the concept that the condition of your house reflects important things about you that need to be addressed. As I have already stated, it's not about the house. Nor is it about working harder or faster or even smarter. The smog of clutter around you will begin to lift as fresh thoughts and feelings sweep into your life.

Working to alter the condition of the house will force you to examine and change what is going on there in relation to yourself. Its condition won't permanently change until you have addressed some of these important basics.

Once you do, the house will be automatically transformed just as mysteriously as it became a mess—because you have been transformed. Then some morning, when you are sitting in your neat house sipping tea, your distressed neighbor may come to your door to escape the chaos she is fighting in her own house. And in the comfort you have created, you may say, "Come right on in! Have a seat, honey. Let me tell you what happened to me."

part 1

understanding the messie mind-set

The secret to change lies in the way we think about messiness and neatness. Somewhere in this section you will find yourself and your way of thinking. Not all types will apply to you, but you will discover some destructive thought patterns that are so much a part of you that they seem normal. They are an important part of your housekeeping problems.

Many women keep neat houses without becoming compulsive, and it's because they think differently from the way you do. You will find out their secret and learn to make it your own.

1

accepting yourself

The gooney bird is funny looking. When it walks it has to lift its large webbed feet high to keep from tripping over them. It also engages in a strange-looking courting ritual. Gooney birds bow and stretch in front of each other. Their large, round bodies are awkward on land, where they court, lay their eggs, and raise their young.

The albatross, on the other hand, is one of the most graceful birds in the world. It has a wingspan of up to twelve feet and can glide on its thin wings longer than any other bird. It is both beautiful and regal.

Few people realize that the gooney bird and the albatross are the same bird with different names. On land it is the gooney bird, ungainly and inept. In the air it is the albatross, king of the sky.

Messies are like this bird. In the area of organization, we are at our weakest, floundering in our attempts to be neat. Like the gooney bird, we have no way to avoid functioning in our weak area. But like the albatross, we do have our sky.

Messies function beautifully in many ways, soaring easily in our areas of strength. While we struggle to improve in the organizational area, we find satisfaction as we soar in other areas.

Messies, however, usually don't see the beautiful side of themselves. All they see is the gooney bird. And they don't like what they see. As a result, Messies treat themselves badly. They're not very nice to themselves, not very nice at all. This is not evident at first, however. Messies are vibrant people who seem to participate in life to the hilt. They are very particular about their personal belongings, and to an extent they are particular about themselves as well. Many of them appear to be happy, well-adjusted people. In many ways they are.

Further examination, however, brings another underlying pattern to the surface. In hundreds of ways a day, Messies, because of the way they think, treat themselves like second-class people.

For Messies, much of life goes on in the mind, so they don't like to be bothered with the day-to-day details of life. As a result, they put up with dripping plumbing and broken appliances because getting them fixed is too much trouble or they need to clean up to let the plumber in. They live without enough light in important areas of the home because correcting the problem is more of a bother than living with it.

On the other hand, Messies always have good intentions. They keep old clothes, convinced that someday they will mend or update them. They have stashes of greeting cards they purchased but never got around to sending.

Messies are forgetful, so they keep everything out where they can see it. If they put it away, they know they'll forget to do it. They blow their noses on toilet paper instead of tissues because they keep forgetting to buy Kleenex. They have too few clocks, mirrors, and trash cans because they never think to buy them.

Messies are perfectionists, so they live in clutter and chaos because there's never enough time to do everything according to their high standards.

Messies are impulsive and live in the moment, so when they decide to bake something special at the last minute, they rarely have the ingredients the recipe calls for.

Messies are impatient, so they use salt, pepper, and sugar from the original containers because transferring them to salt and pepper shakers or a sugar bowl takes too much time.

People's lives have dark places as well as bright ones, difficulties as well as abilities. The combination makes us unique.

In hundreds of ways Messies do without. The old-fashioned way of doing things, so popular with Messies, is just another systematic way of doing without modern conveniences or supplies.

In light of this daily denial of what they need to make life comfortable, it is not surprising that they also deny themselves a place to sit on the sofa because it is covered with stuff. They deny themselves companionship because they can't invite guests over with the house the way it is. They sometimes sleep on the floor because the bed is piled with clothes they haven't had time to put away.

But Messies are used to self-denial. They do without or make do. Instead of recognizing the problem, they adjust to it. And they are very good at it. Many even take pride in their make-do approach. They are happy to show you how they do without the things other people who recognize their worth and dignity provide for themselves.

Ultimately, Messies deny themselves a life of serenity and beauty. They insult themselves with disorganization on such a regular basis that they are unaware of it. The messy house is just part of the picture of a person who consistently abuses herself. Messiness is just the top of a very deep pile of problems. At its heart, messiness is a problem of self-neglect.

The First Step

To put an end to this pattern of denial, Messies must first stop fighting themselves. If we get angry at ourselves and go to war against certain character traits every time we see them, we only give them the energy to stay. *Star Trek* fans may remember the story called "The Empath" in which Mr. Spock and Captain Kirk were surrounded by a force field that kept them from helping Dr. McCoy, who was in trouble. The more they struggled to get out, the stronger the force field became because it gained strength from the energy of their struggle. When Mr. Spock realized this and stopped struggling, the force field lost its power to restrain them.

Like Mr. Spock, the more we struggle against the force that holds us back, the stronger the force gets. Unless we accept ourselves and our habits and our lives as they are *now*, we will never overcome the negative forces.

When it first dawns on you what has been happening, you may be angry at yourself, the house, or the thoughts that got you in this fix. Don't fight the anger; it is part of the picture too and must be accepted. It may be what spurs you to move forward. When it has done its work, you can get back to self-acceptance.

I cannot overemphasize the importance of self-acceptance. We are people of dignity. We love order and beauty. We are worthwhile. Zig Ziglar tells of a painting by Rembrandt that sold for over a million dollars. Ziglar wondered why the price was so high. Is paint that expensive? Does canvas cost a lot? Of course not. The value of the painting was twofold:

1. It was painted by a master.
2. It is one of a kind.

This reminds us of our own value. We were painted, shadows and highlights, by a master painter who "does all things well," who made both the albatross and the gooney bird parts of us. We are wonderful because we come from his hand.

Like Rembrandt's painting, we too are unique. No one else has our exact makeup, our strengths and weaknesses, shadows and highlights. Rembrandt's paintings contain a lot of shadow, but it enhances their beauty. People's lives have dark places as well as bright ones, difficulties as well as abilities. It is fine to have both. The combination makes us unique.

Why Not?

Most of the time when I talk to people about Messies Anonymous they know only too well why someone would want to change her house. Occasionally, however, on a radio talk show or in an interview for a newspaper, someone will ask why people should be concerned about getting their houses in order.

My best answer to that question is another question: Why not?

Why not have a lovely home that encourages all who enter? Why not be among those who are thrilled to invite people over on the spur of the moment? Why not be the person to whom people say, "Your house is so lovely!" Why not have people over for meals without working yourself to death to get ready? Why not have a house that raises your self-esteem rather than tears it down? Why not have a house filled with your favorite colors and accents? Why not have a house that reflects the peace and grace of God so that others love to come over to hear about him? Why not have a house in which you can read or pray without feeling guilty because you're not cleaning? The question is not why should we have a nice house. The real question is *why not*?

Assess the Mess

1. List all the ways you deny yourself, even those you think of as frugality. They will not all come to mind at once (you may be so used to living with them that none come

to mind at all), so turn down the corner of this page so you can find it easily to add to the list. (Yes! I did say turn down the corner of the page. I know it may bother you to mess up the book, but you will be writing in it anyway, so it won't matter. Yes! I did say write in it. Oh, all right, if you must, insert a paper here to write on, but you'd better paper clip it. In the lives of Messies, things move on their own.)

a.

b.

c.

2. If money were no object, what things around the house would you upgrade? What would you buy that you have been denying yourself? Jot them down quickly and add others as you recognize changes you would like to make.

a.

b.

c.

3. List the characteristics, both albatross and gooney bird, that combine to make you unique.

a. (albatross)

b. (albatross)

c. (albatross)

d. (gooney bird)

e. (gooney bird)

f. (gooney bird)

4. Why do you think Messies deny themselves?

2

the saver messie

"If you don't want it, give it to Susan. She takes everything."

It's true. Susan hates to see things go to waste, and she's sure she'll find a use for them, at least most of them—someday. So her basement, attic, garage, and every spare corner are crammed with things no one else wants. Susan's not sure she wants them either, but she doesn't dare get rid of them. If she throws something away, she is sure she will need it the next day. And besides, it's too late to start saying no to people's offers. They might think she is ungrateful. What's a saver to do? Buy a bigger house?

Susan's obsession with saving comes from her desire always to have whatever she or anyone else needs. Her mentality is not uncommon, but it's only one of the many mind-sets that lead to uncontrolled saving.

Messies have very real reasons for doing what they do. And they feel very strongly about their reasons. Messies are generally logical and intelligent people. Although they may not like the disorganized lifestyle and the problems it causes, the things they do that keep it that way are consistent with how they think.

Messies have problems in three basic areas: saving too much, cluttering, and wasting time. As we look at these areas in the next three chapters, put a check beside the thinking patterns that fit you.

Saving

1. **Scarcity.** Messies live on the verge of the next Great Depression. It has nothing to do with the state of the economy. Many people who have always lived in affluence hoard things because they fear, emotionally if not intellectually, that they will not have enough in the future. Is this a factor in your thinking?

2. **Hobby.** Some people so love saving that they develop specialties. Wealthy people do this with art or other collections. People of ordinary means love to collect too. They collect bottles, antiques, figurines, and so on. It gives them something to talk about, gives them something to do on vacation, and puts them in contact with friends and acquaintances they would not otherwise have. Sometimes it takes the form of gathering information on various subjects, either by clipping articles or printing them off the Internet.

Messies collect too many things, the wrong kind of things, and just junk. They are pack rats. Does collecting affect your house negatively?

3. **Comfort.** Some Messies find comfort in having a lot of belongings. They feel better when they have books, boxes, bottles, papers, clothes, and food around the house. Perhaps things are so out of order that having many of the same item gives them some assurance that they will be able to find at least one when they need it.

But it is more than that. These things become their friends, often substituting for real people who are being squeezed out of their lives by the clutter. Do you find comfort in things?

4. **One-of-a-kind things.** Some things are unique, so we reason, "If I don't buy this rabbit-shaped butter mold now, I may never see one again. If I want it, I had better get it." Have you ever done this type of gathering?

5. **Guilt.** Benjamin Franklin did much to set the tone for saving. *Poor Richard's Almanac* is full of catchy sayings about it. His admonitions have followed us through history. Certainly wanton wastefulness is a bad idea. So is wanton saving, but nobody has made a slogan about that. What sayings have you built your life on? Two that are applicable to our situation are "Waste not, want not" and "A penny saved is a penny earned."

> Wanton wastefulness is a bad idea. So is wanton saving, but nobody has made a slogan about that.

What other slogans have set the stage for your over-collecting? Do you hear the echo of your mother, grand-mother, or other family members warning you not to let go of anything? Do you ever feel guilty for doing it?

6. **Bargains.** The mantel clock was such a bargain she had to get it. Only a fool would pass up such an opportunity. But she didn't have a mantel—or any other place to put it. It is evidence of her crafty buying skills, so she keeps it as a trophy. Do you buy things you don't need simply because they are cheap?

7. **Gratitude.** The things we keep may be birthday or wedding gifts from relatives or secondhand junk from a friend, but they have two things in common: they are free, and they are associated with someone we love or care about. This makes them impossible to part with. They appeal to both our frugality and sentimentality. We feel that we have to take them and, what's more, that we have to keep them. Do you have difficulty getting rid of useless gifts?

8. **Sentimentality.** Messies are afraid they will forget the past. Many do have poor memories. They need to be able to touch and hold things from the past to keep their memories alive. Messies take multiple snapshots, sometimes compul-

sively, to capture the present for posterity. Do you save to keep the past alive?

9. **Anthropomorphism.** No one except a Messie can fully understand the feeling that objects have a life of their own. The life they have is usually part of the life of the person who owned them. If I get rid of something meaningful to me, I feel as if I am giving away part of myself. Even worse, if I get rid of something that has belonged to someone meaningful to me, I feel that I am giving away part of them and betraying their memory. It is more a feeling than a thought. Are you stymied because your things are somehow a little bit alive and you must nurture them?

> When you acquire things that don't satisfy your need, no amount is ever enough.

When it came time for me to give away my last maternity dress, I put it on the bed each day so it could lie in state. I needed to do that for me to get used to the idea that it was going to leave my house and for it to get used to the idea that it was leaving. When Messies get rid of something, they often feel they must find a good home for it and check up on how it is getting along. This is difficult to do, so we decide it is easier to just keep things. Do you sometimes feel that things have feelings?

10. **Fear.** "What if the IRS should audit? I need to keep everything I might ever need!" It is true that everyone needs to keep records for tax purposes, but the reality is that if we keep all the stuff we're afraid to throw away, we won't be able to find the old income tax forms, much less the receipts and records that go with them, if we ever need them. We are afraid we will need receipts for the credit cards or for the department store or the light company or something. It is certainly a good idea to have what we need for these occasions, but the unreasonable fear that causes us to keep too much is as much trouble as keeping too little. The irony is that we keep so much that if we ever did need something, it would be impossible to find, buried in unnecessary papers. Do you keep

all records just in case you will be asked to produce some of them sometime? Have you ever needed them?

11. **Procrastination.** Some Messies put off getting rid of things that require action. Every day the mailman delivers a new batch of problems for Messies. They don't want to pay the bills until the due date, so they let them pile up. They don't want to take the time right now to read the junk mail, so they keep it. They want to save the magazine for a more relaxing day, so they keep it. After only a few days they have a box full of "to do" reading. Then the boxes start piling up. Clutter is a pile of unmade decisions.

A procrastinating Messie told me that he wishes for a fire to get rid of the clutter. That way he could blame God, not himself, that some things never got done. Does procrastination cause clutter in your life?

12. **Value.** You and I both know that it is not right to get rid of things that have worth. Books and magazines contain valuable ideas. The pen is mightier than the sword. Messies believe they have power at their fingertips in this printed material. It doesn't matter to them that some of those textbooks are so old that the ideas are long outdated. Nor does it matter that most of the books are packed away, and they don't know where they are and can't remember what's in them. Their value is more imaginary than real.

Messies are unreasonably hopeful when it comes to the future value of things. They wildly imagine that some obscure item will become valuable. They even envision wild stories the neighbors will tell their children when it happens—"See that house over there? The person who lived in it kept almost everything he ever owned. One day in his basement he came across a mint condition first copy of a Superman comic book. That thing brought two million dollars at an auction. Now he's moved away to a mansion. He used to be as poor as a church mouse; now he's on easy street. I sure wish I had been as wise as he was and kept everything I ever laid my hands on."

Many Messies collect things for the same reason others buy lottery tickets. They hope one day to strike it rich. Are you collecting because you think your items have or will have great value? Are the things you collect worth the trouble of living with them? What are they costing you on a daily basis to live with?

Messies collect things for the same reason others buy lottery tickets. They hope one day to strike it rich.

13. **Posterity.** There is a great temptation to keep things for the grandchildren—"They don't make toys as good as the ones I bought for my children. What a thrill for little Billy to play with the bulldozer his dad had at his age." And on it goes. Are you keeping things for posterity?

14. **Mother of the world.** For reasons discussed later in the book, Messies feel responsible for the whole world's well-being. If anyone else in the neighborhood needs something, we think they should be able to come to us and get it. We save old catalogs just in case a neighbor's child needs to get pictures for a school poster. The little kid who wants scrap wood for his project can find it at our house.

Why don't these kids' folks have the things they need? Because they are providing an orderly and clutter-free home, so the kids will be spared the confusion that exists at ours. Do you think you must be ready to provide for the unpredictable needs of others?

15. **Habit.** We have gotten so used to keeping things that we no longer bother to make a choice about them. If someone puts a flyer on our windshield, we keep it. If we are sent a coupon in the mail, we keep it. If the kids bring home stuff from school, we keep it all. When we receive a letter, we even keep the empty envelope. With few exceptions, we keep everything that comes to our hands. It is our way of life. Do you keep things without thinking about whether or not you really need them?

16. **Creativity.** Those who perceive themselves as creative like to find creative uses for junk. They cut up a bleach bottle and use it to hold clothespins on the clothesline. They cut the feet off ruined panty hose and fill them with soap sliv-

ers for bathing. And they save things they don't have a use for just in case they think of one. They don't know what to do with all their old butter tubs, but they are too good to throw away.

I once caught myself wanting to save the underwires that I had removed from bras. I thought about painting them and making Christmas ornaments. Now really! Who wants bra underwire Christmas ornaments? But such is our desire to save for creativity. It is part of the Messie's make-do mentality. Do you have the creative urge to make things from junk?

17. **Rebellion.** If someone got rid of your things when you were a child, perhaps you keep stuff to show that you now have power over your own things. In this case, the more your mom or husband urges you to get rid of things, the more determined you are to keep them. Now that you are grown up, you can clutter to your heart's content and no one can stop you. Are you a rebellious clutterer?

18. **Satisfaction.** Some people try to get something from their belongings that belongings were never meant to give. Because people are unfulfilled and cannot find satisfaction, they keep gathering more and more stuff, hoping that one day it will satisfy them. But it never does. Look at the word fulfilled. It means "filled full." They think that if they get filled full enough they will feel fulfilled. The truth is, when you acquire things that don't satisfy your need, no amount is ever enough. Are you looking for satisfaction in the things you save?

19. **Holidays.** The holidays, traditionally, are times of over-doing. People overeat, overbuy, overcelebrate, and overwork. It is not surprising that many people also overdo on holiday collecting. The stores are full of decorations that convince us we need every one. Collectors reason that they can pass them to their grandchildren if they get too many. This kind of collecting is hard to resist for sentimental Messies. Do you overbuy during the holidays?

"I can't seem to chip away at my own junk buildup," wrote Roberta Katchen Stein in the *Chicago Tribune* (July 29, 1984).

"I cling to my backlog of possessions as zealously as Peter Pan stuck to his shadow."

If you and your possessions are inseparable, it's time to reassess your situation.

Hoarding

Some of the people who read this book will fall into a category of saving behavior beyond what is common among Messies. These people have the same characteristics as those mentioned above; however, they save things to such a great degree that it falls into a category all its own. We call that category hoarding. For purposes of discussion, we will call the folks who fall into this group *hoarders*.

Let me hasten to mention that the word *hoarders* is not meant as finger pointing. Those who hoard are usually very fine people who have many good characteristics. They are often quite intelligent, have good values, are pleasant to be with, are hard workers, and are overall contributors to society. People who hoard are not crazy. They have, however, lost control of a very important area of their lives. The reason I stress these positive points is that hoarding carries with it a lot of shame and brings a lot of condemnation from society and sometimes from governmental agencies.

It was not until the late 1980s that hoarding began to be studied. Randy Frost of Smith College, a psychologist and leading pioneer in the field, recounts that it was a student's question in a psychology class on obsessive-compulsive disorders that pointed out the fact that hoarding was a neglected area of study. Since then, researchers have begun to study the problem.

Although hoarding is usually studied in the obsessive-compulsive disorder context, it does not follow the patterns of excessive hand-washing and other more well-known behavior rituals. One of the differences is that the person who collects is usually not distressed by the accumulation of possessions the way people with other kinds of obsessive-compulsive disorders are. Typically, they reject offers of help.

Gathering pets, often cats, is common. Hoarders find comfort, enjoyment, even safety from having their things around them or safely stored elsewhere. They may, however, become distressed with the results of their hoarding. Frequently, they become reclusive in order to avoid unpleasant consequences. These consequences may occur when their family puts pressure on them to change, when social services threaten to remove children from the home, when the landlord threatens eviction, when city health officials threaten punitive action, or when life becomes too complicated because of their inability to function in the home. Under these circumstances, they may be willing to accept help or, in some cases, even ask for help in changing.

Even then, however, the hoarder finds it difficult to give up cherished belongings. Their chief discomfort comes from the fear they feel if they are asked to part with their things. They want to solve the problem without letting go of them. To overcome these barriers, various avenues of help are possible. Remember, hoarding is not intrinsically morally wrong or illegal. It is important to respect the hoarder's autonomy as much as the circumstances will allow. Of course, sometimes legal, health, safety, or even personal factors don't give a lot of leeway in this area.

- The hoarder may consent to work with family and friends if there is a clear understanding of what the hoarder is willing and not willing to discard or change. Experience indicates that those who help a hoarder in this way should have a clear, preferably written, "contract" to guide them as they work with the hoarder's belongings. My twenty-four-page booklet on the self-help approach called *I've Got to Get Rid of This Stuff* is available from Messies Anonymous (www.messies.com). In the book *Conquering Chronic Disorganization*, Judith Kolberg outlines an excellent "battle plan" for utilizing outside help in seriously disorganized homes. It may easily be adapted to helping a hoarder.

- Mental health professionals with success in the area of treating hoarding may be helpful. Seek out behavioral psychologists who focus on the goal of behavior change. Medication used for other obsessive-compulsive disorders is sometimes helpful.
- Hoarding may have several causes. For help with hoarding behavior that may be related to obsessive-compulsive disorders, call the Obsessive-Compulsive Foundation in Milford, Connecticut, at (203) 878-5669.
- Professional organizers with training in the area of hoarding are available for guidance. The National Study Group on Chronic Disorganization, associated with the National Association of Professional Organizers (www.napo.net), is probably the best resource for help in this area.

Assess the Mess

1. List the factors mentioned in this chapter that cause you to save too much. Add any others that you have thought of.

   a.
   b.
   c.
   d.

2. Give examples of how these factors affect you. Do you lose things in the multitude of belongings? Do you keep people out? Do you turn down invitations because you have to stay home and organize?

   a.
   b.
   c.
   d.

3. Do you see yourself (or someone you love) as a serious hoarder? If so, list several steps you will take to begin to address the problem.

a.

b.

c.

d.

the clutterer messie

Connie leaves piles of clothes all over the house. It used to drive her mother crazy, then her roommates, and now her husband. They are all amazed that she manages to look good whenever she goes out. They can't figure out why she doesn't always look as if she just crawled out of the dirty clothes hamper. But there's a method to Connie's madness. What no one understands is that it's the piles that keep Connie from looking that way. They are her way of sorting her wardrobe. Since she's perfectionistic in her own way, she can't bear the idea of putting once-worn clothes back in the closet where they might contaminate the clean clothes. Or she might forget they are not perfectly fresh. But neither does she want to put them with the dirty clothes because she might have to wear them again before she does the laundry.

So the piles work well for Connie. Connie is working hard to do everything right, but it sure leaves a mess.

There are, of course, more sensible solutions to Connie's dilemma, but because no one understands the way she thinks, no one can help her. And, of course, there are many other reasons why people clutter their surroundings.

1. **Poor memory.** People who have a poor memory are afraid to put things away because they will forget where they are or even that they have them.

2. **No place to put things away.** The house is small, storage space is scarce, and there is already too much stuff in the storage places. In short, the stuff is spilling over because there's too much of it. Messies find it difficult to know what storage pieces are needed, and they don't think of buying things like cabinets and shelves. Their make-do mentality is one of the reasons they have no place to put things.

3. **Energy conservation.** Messies believe in production-line straightening. We don't put away one little thing at a time. It's not efficient. So we let things pile up. When we designate a time, we put everything away all at once. While we are waiting to start the assembly line, the house is a wreck.

4. **Serendipitous benefit.** Somewhere, sometime the clutterer heard a story about someone who was united with long-lost relatives through a set of unlikely circumstances. Perhaps a friend was visiting a clutterer who had snapshots lying on the lamp table. The friend glanced at a photo and said, "That man looks like my uncle, Bernie Stein, who was killed in Germany during the war." "Why, that's Sam Stein!" the photo owner says. "He and his dad, Bernie, run a deli in Miami Beach! Bernie isn't dead! He's alive and well!" The clutterer is thrilled that he has helped reunite these family members. And it was all because he left out his snapshots. Who says leaving clutter out is not a good idea? Magical fantasies abound in the imaginative Messie mind.

5. **To keep people away.** The cluttered house is an excuse to keep people out. When our house is too cluttered to en-

tertain, we have a reason for not allowing visitors to use up our time. Even though some disorganized people want to entertain, they find it very difficult to do so.

6. **Love.** We love to see our nice things. Why should we put them away? Of course, some are buried out of sight.

7. **Distractions.** The distractible person starts a job and then quits, leaving a bunch of stuff undone. She puts something down without realizing it and doesn't remember where. She means to straighten things, but something else intrudes. Distractibility is a major contributor to messiness.

> Messies believe in production-line straightening. But while we are waiting to start the assembly line, the house is a wreck.

8. **Defines personality.** Being a Messie has certain advantages. One of them is that it makes us unique. We can make jokes about clutter. Others can tease us about it. We tell ourselves that being messy is a superior way of life. It is part of our self-concept. Some of us have signs on our desks (usually buried) that say, "A clean desk is a sign of a sick mind."

9. **Defines relationships.** Messiness plays an important part in some relationships. The messy person takes the place of the child even if she is an adult. Her mother, mother-in-law, husband, roommate, or some other figure takes the place of the parent. The messy person and the "parent" establish part of their relationship around the person's messiness. The "parent" fusses at the "child." The "child" rebels or is sorry. Or both. The relationship is a negative one, but it is one they both understand. If the messy person were to change tomorrow, how would they relate?

10. **Attracts attention.** Occasionally the messy lifestyle gets much-wanted attention. Well-meaning friends help us clean. They suggest ways of improving. All this attention would disappear if the messiness disappeared.

11. **Family problems.** People who live in cluttered houses probably aren't the only clutterers. If they begin to live a

clutter-free life, there is no telling what conflicts might arise in the family. Other family members will want to continue leaving their shoes in the living room and their books on the dining room table. They already complain about having to put away a few of their things. Some people live cluttered lives to keep from upsetting the family.

12. **Executive dysfunction.** Our more organized sisters have a natural knack for organizing. When they look at a situation that needs organizing, the steps for doing the job form automatically in their brains. Those with executive dysfunction, an inborn inability to execute organizational activities easily, do not have that same experience. They have trouble knowing where to begin and how to proceed. It is with difficulty that they feel their way along. The choices they make may not be the best. Because of the difficulties, the job becomes unpleasant and discouraging. Sometimes they stop in the middle or avoid starting another similar activity, even when it cries out to be done.

One of the differences between organized people and Messies may be that Messies sort groups into smaller, more specific groups. For them, every item has its own special features and, therefore, does not belong in a group with others that are a little different. Successful organizers tend to group things more broadly. They perceive how items relate. They store and label these broader groups for easy retrieval. This makes for much more successful housekeeping because the person does not have to deal with the unimportant details you get when you have smaller groupings.

Very little has been studied in this area, but natural organizational ability is certainly a factor to consider. Those who experience executive dysfunction vaguely sense that there is something different about their natural ability to organize. All is not hopeless, however. Learning and applying the skills that come naturally to others will move us confidently in the right direction. It may take extra effort, but it will definitely work.

Assess the Mess

List the factors mentioned in this chapter that contribute to your habit of cluttering. Add others that you have thought of. Give examples of how they affect your life.

   1.

   2.

   3.

   4.

   5.

   6.

4

the time-waster messie

Tammy, like many Messies, is an optimistic person. One thing she is optimistic about is her time use. She always thinks she will be able to be on time, but it doesn't work out that way. She always underestimates how long it takes to do things. For twenty years it has taken her an hour to get ready for work in the morning. Nevertheless, every morning she optimistically thinks she can cut the time to forty-five minutes if she just hurries a little bit, so she sleeps an extra fifteen minutes. But every morning for twenty years she has been fifteen minutes late for work. Because she is always running late, she never has time to put the breakfast dishes in the dishwasher, straighten the bathroom, or hang up the clothes she decided not to wear. Tammy has one of the classic characteristics of a time waster. And there are others.

1. **Poor sense of passing time.** Many Messies have no sense of how long it takes to do things. They may agree to do something without realizing they are humanly incapable of accomplishing it in the prescribed amount of time. Some

don't even wear watches. They are not concerned about the timing of things, only about the doing. If they are distractible as well, they do not feel the flow of time in the way a nondistractible person does. The constant misjudgment of time is a sure symptom of the Messie mind-set.

> The unwillingness to make decisions about our own priorities and values is a form of laziness.

2. **Sense of importance.** Important people are busy people. They pack their schedules full to assure themselves of their own importance. People sometimes kill themselves with the idea that they are very important people doing very important work. A minister who had had several heart attacks but continued to keep a horrendously heavy schedule told a class of young seminary students that he was going to burn out for God. The pride with which he told the story led some students to wonder if he were not burning out for his own ego's sake. Sometimes our motives may surprise us.

3. **Unwilling to take control.** Some people are addicted to having others tell them what to do. They rarely schedule anything for themselves or decide anything for themselves. Instead, they go with the flow by waiting for parents, spouses, children, or God to tell them what to do. This leads to chaos because everyone has a different idea about what the Messie should be doing. We all have plenty of pressure without adding to it by allowing others to take control of our lives.

A favorite theme of C. S. Lewis, author of the Chronicles of Narnia, is that only lazy people work hard. The unwillingness to make decisions about our own priorities and values is a form of laziness, and it results in a frantic life of always trying to meet the many demands to which we have haphazardly opened the door.

Sometimes Christians even take a sort of Ouija board approach. They set up a system of signs for God and expect him to show his guidance according to their rules. Perhaps it is God's will for them to set up their own thoughtful schedules and stick to them.

Knowing Makes a Difference

Knowing why we keep too much stuff, leave things around, and schedule our lives poorly is the first step toward change. Only when we realize what thoughts are guiding our actions can we begin to counteract them. To change our actions, we must change our thoughts. Many of the thoughts that guide our lives are good thoughts. They just don't work in our situation. Others are reasonable if not taken to the extreme to which we take them. And some are not as good as we thought when we first embraced them.

> Only lazy people work hard.

At the circus you may see a six-thousand-pound elephant tethered to a small stake with a thin rope. With his great strength, he could easily pull the stake out or break the rope, but he doesn't know he can. As a baby, the elephant was tied strongly to an immovable object. He tried and tried to get loose but never could. Finally convinced that elephants tied to a stake cannot get loose, he stopped trying. Even though he is perfectly able to get away now, he doesn't try anymore. He lives by an idea he formed a long time ago. It no longer applies to his situation, but he sticks by it anyway. If someone who knew elephant talk would whisper to him that he doesn't have to live by the idea he formed as a baby, do you think he would throw over his old idea? I think so. If he could see the life possible for him, I think he would choose freedom.

Most of our beliefs were set by the time we were twelve years old. Why are we willing to continue living by the beliefs of a twelve-year-old? Now that we are adults and know the ideas that motivate us to be messy, we can evaluate them and decide what we want to do with them.

Assess the Mess

List the factors that cause you to waste time. Add any of your own that you have thought of. Give examples of how they affect your life.

1.
2.
3.
4.
5.

5

ADD adds to the problem

ADD and disorganization go hand in hand. Experts took a long time to realize that attention deficit disorder (ADD) affects adults as well as children. And one of the chief characteristics of people with ADD is disorganization. According to Dale Jordan in *Attention Deficit Disorder*, disorganization is the "earmark of adult attention deficit disorder." Thom Hartmann concurs in *ADD Success Stories*, "People with ADD are often disorganized and cluttered, and can benefit tremendously from learning organizational strategies that teach them how to impose order and systems on their schooling or work." Sari Solden in *Women with Attention Deficit Disorder* states that "disorganization in one form or another is the subject that most women with ADD talk about the most in counseling."

Obviously, not everybody who has a problem with disorganization has attention deficit disorder. However, it is probably true that, with little exception, everybody with attention deficit disorder struggles to stay organized.

How It All Starts

Some Messie children with ADD can hold the details of their lives together in the early years. They may seem a little dippy or dreamy. But life is simpler, and Mom helps keep their act together. The problem shows up later as life becomes more complicated.

For others the business of being disorganized shows up early. Some people seem to be born disorganized. Nobody taught them slovenliness, but even as kids they are experts. Their scatterbrained behavior leaves the family in turmoil. Adults have methods of motivating the mini-Messie to orderliness but with varying degrees of success.

Mary's room is always a shambles. Her mom redecorated it, hoping Mary would care more about the room and keep it neat. It didn't work.

Little Jack regularly forgets to turn in his homework. Actually, he doesn't forget; he can't find it. It's in his book bag or locker, he thinks—maybe. If you could see the book bag you would know why he's not sure. The family takes a "you're going to live with the consequences of your actions" approach after trying everything else. They hope that if he fails often enough, he will be cured forever.

Ronny's mom sends him to the store to buy something only when she cannot find anyone else to go. All the time he is gone she wonders: Will he lose the money on the way? Will he remember what he went for? Will he lose the change or the package on the way home? Will he meet a friend and forget to come home at all?

All over the country children like these, through no effort or fault of their own, are driving their parents and teachers crazy. What the parents may not realize is that these children are more baffled than the parents about what the problem is. To the children the situation looks much different; they find themselves inexplicably in trouble about things they were unaware they were doing wrong.

Mary's room, though a shambles in her mother's eyes, is not offensive to Mary. She hardly notices how it looks, so she has a hard time understanding her mother's concern. As a matter of fact, when her mother points out the messy condition, Mary has a hard time understanding how it got that way. Whenever her mother gets the room straightened, it seems to disorganize itself the minute Mary walks in.

Jack's book bag and locker are a shambles. Nobody, not even a responsible adult, could use them successfully. His classmates have divider notebooks and are very neat. Jack's papers are wrinkled masses amid his jumble of books. How his classmates keep things in order is a mystery to him. Being organized looks like a wonderful way of life, but he feels it is beyond his ability. His teachers and parents tell him it is easy and necessary to use a divider notebook. His father even bought one and set it up for him. But it wasn't long before the notebook was lost and his papers were again crumpled in the corners of his locker and book bag.

Ronny is keenly aware that he loses things, but he doesn't know why. It seems to him that people must be taking his things or moving them around secretly. When he leaves something out on a table, it disappears without a trace, and he does not know where it went. Sometimes the item never comes back, and sometimes it reappears as mysteriously as it left. His parents, who are on his case about keeping up with his things, do not realize that all of this is confusing, frightening, and frustrating. Ronny has no control over his things, and he doesn't know how to get control. His things seem to have a life of their own. His parents' hassling just adds further stress to this already stressful situation.

What Is the Problem?

Teachers say these children need self-discipline. Psychologists say they need motivation. Doctors say they are immature. Parents oscillate between all three evaluations and their own despair. In the meantime, the offending children are trying to find a way to live in this confusing world. It may seem to others that they don't care, but this is usually not true. It's just that caring doesn't bring any relief. It just adds to the stress. So they go on as best they can. Sometimes their parents do help them by setting up an organizational system that alleviates the problem somewhat. Sometimes they compensate well, but for most the general problem remains the same. It doesn't help when adults treat them as though they are dumb or bad. Sometimes the children believe the adults may be right.

Children like these all over the country may be suffering from some form of attention deficit disorder, a term that has come into common use since about 1980 but has been observed and written about since the seventeenth century. Previously, such terms as hyperactivity and minimum brain dysfunction were used to describe difficulty with concentration and attention span. There are as many as six varieties of ADD, but two varieties of ADD are the most common and are most commonly known: ADD with hyperactivity and ADD without hyperactivity.

In both cases the child is distractible (daydreams and has trouble ignoring distractions while trying to do a task), has organizational struggles with time and space (can't carry out steps of an organizing job), has a poor attention span especially for routine tasks (doesn't finish jobs or stick with them to the end, but can attend to tasks which capture his interest), is impulsive (acts, talks, or makes decisions without thinking or self-restraint), and has poor social sense (has trouble making and keeping friends because of inappropriate behavior). Those who have hyperactivity in addition to ADD are excessively active.

What Causes These Problems?

About 7 percent of the population has ADD. Five times more boys are diagnosed with it than girls, although it is probably equally distributed across gender lines. More are diagnosed who are hyperactive or engage in negative behavior. Those who are not hyperactive do not cause as many problems and are often overlooked. Less than 2 percent receive medication. According to *The Journal of the American Medical Association*, there is no evidence that ADD is overdiagnosed in our society.

The cause of ADD is attributed to a number of factors. For some, it is caused by a problem with chemicals in the brain called neurotransmitters, which coordinate and regulate functions and behaviors. A slight deficiency in these neurotransmitters can cause the lack of attention that is characteristic of ADD and leads to messiness and disorganization.

Genetics play a big part. ADD tends to run in families. In his excellent book *Healing ADD,* Dr. Daniel G. Amen states that if one parent has ADD, the child has a 60 percent chance of having it. If a child has two parents with it, the chances rise to 85 to 90 percent. Often there is a strong familial history of symptoms.

Other factors have been examined. Head injury can precipitate it. Since early in the history of ADD, diet has been suggested as a part of the problem and solution. Even inner ear problems have been targeted for study.

Another factor in ADD may be a problem relating to the muscular and neurological function of the eye. Just as some children (and adults) have responded to dietary change, some have responded to visual training by an optometrist who is a visual specialist. These approaches work with varying effectiveness and may be considered when a person is looking for help with managing this problem. For most, however, they will not be the major avenue of help.

Sleep disorders also seem to be associated with ADD. Bedwetting, grinding of teeth, and sleepwalking or talking may be indications of a sleep disorder. These disorders are more common among the ADD population than the general public. One theory is that people who do not experience the natural sleep cycle, including the proper REM sleep cycle at night, must tune in and out during the day to get what other people get at night. The daytime symptoms of a person with a sleep disorder are similar to the symptoms of ADD. How sleep problems relate to ADD is unclear and will require further study.

Since ADD is a neurological problem with a biological basis, medication plays an important part in the solution. Since ADD may be caused by a variety of things, and there are several types of ADD, careful evaluation by a competent expert is necessary to know which medication is appropriate. It is not uncommon for parents and patients alike to resist the taking of medication for ADD. Properly administered, medications have little potential for abuse. Careful study of the results of medication indicates that those who are properly treated with the correct medication and dosages are at lower risk for drug abuse. For most, untreated ADD has worse side effects than medication.

Not all attention deficits are caused by true ADD. Illegal drug use, side effects from certain types of prescribed medications, psychological problems, and a myriad of other problems need to be eliminated when diagnosing ADD.

Getting through the Teen Years

As ADD children reach puberty, the developmental lag tends to close. The problem seems to solve itself to some degree. But it does not solve itself completely. Some of the ADD characteristics of distractibility, poor attention control, impulsiveness, and sometimes immature social behavior remain.

Teenagers have a hard enough time with new distractions in the areas of physical and social development and self-esteem. A teenager with attention deficit disorder can be expected to have a more turbulent time than most. Teens with this problem have had many negative experiences because of their own confusion about the condition and because of the misunderstanding of other people. Teenagers with ADD have a higher incidence of academic problems, social problems, problems with drug and alcohol abuse, and even trouble with the law. Problems with messiness and disorganization are just two of the many complications of ADD.

The ADD Adult

As the ADD child grows into puberty, approximately 25 to 50 percent seem to outgrow the symptoms of ADD. This percentage may be inflated, however. Hyperactivity does tend to lessen markedly, but many other symptoms of the disorder remain. Some of the problems that made the child disorganized and messy remain into adulthood. While some symptoms are lessening, the problem is being compounded in other ways because the adult's life is so much more complex than the child's.

Sometimes the problem does not surface until the child becomes an adult, especially if the person is particularly intelligent. Mann and Greenspan, writing in *The Journal of Psychiatry*, say that the disorder is difficult to diagnose in an adult.

> We suspect that many children with either mild or moderate attention difficulties, coupled with an unusual degree of creativity, intelligence and capacity for interpersonal relationships . . . do not experience manifest psychiatric difficulties until they encounter the stresses of adult life.

This is why many women who have been able to hold their lives together through childhood and the teen years begin to falter when they have their own home and family to care for. Some falter after having one child, some after two or more. Each has a different level of ability depending on the severity of her ADD. Each person hits the wall of ADD at a different time. Sometimes it is when she takes her own child in for an ADD evaluation that she begins to wake up to the possibility that this may have been her problem for many years.

In my case, I faltered immediately after college. Until that time I was a little scatterbrained and spacey, but I got good support from home because it was always organized. I could handle my college schedule and my college room. But anything more than that (home, husband, work, bills, mail, cooking, children) was way too much, as I found out immediately.

> Keeping the house in order is a gargantuan task for a person with this disorder.

Keeping the house in order is a gargantuan task for a person with this disorder. Here are some examples of how it interferes with orderliness:

1. **Poor attention span.** Luci begins a large task, such as the week's laundry. She loads the dirty clothes into the car, drives to the Laundromat, lugs the full baskets to the washer, starts the washer, removes the clothes when they are finished, puts them into the dryer, and removes them when they are dry. By now she's had enough of the laundry job. While her counterparts patiently fold their clean sheets, towels, and underwear and hang the shirts and dresses on hangers, Luci stuffs hers into the basket and goes home. She's had enough of one job for a while. But now she will have to iron the clothes that would have been wrinkle free if she had hung them up straight from the dryer.

The same thing happens when she buys groceries, cooks, or starts a hobby. She has enough attention to get started but not enough to finish. So the one thing that usually goes undone is the cleanup.

· Luci might tackle a big job like cleaning a large closet and run out of persistence right in the middle of it. She leaves the mess in the middle of the floor for her husband to throw back into the closet when he gets tired of seeing it. Now the problem is bigger than it was before.

2. **Distractibility.** Dorothy is constantly pulled away from jobs by the telephone, her children's needs, and her own day-

dreams or interests. She works all day but accomplishes little because she does not go very far in any direction. Knowing she is distractible, she fears she will forget to do something important.

To counter this tendency, she leaves things out to remind her to do them. On the hall table is Joey's progress report, which she must sign and return to school. By the front door is the package she wants to mail and the can of food she wants to take to church for the food basket. On the dining room table are several bills to pay and some flyers she wants to look at.

These fears— losing things, forgetting things, not finishing things, doing the wrong thing, doing nothing—all cause more work.

She often does one thing while thinking about another, which causes forgetfulness. She will be so deep in thought that she will not notice where she puts things or remember whether or not she handled them at all. Or she may leave her child behind as she drives hurriedly on to the next activity.

Dorothy walks off and leaves the kitchen a mess after fixing a sandwich because she is distracted by the food she is going to eat. She may also leave the stove turned on as she walks away. She writes a check and forgets to record it because the clerk distracts her. This amount of distractibility causes a chaotic, disorganized life.

3. **Boredom with routine tasks.** Most housework is nothing if it is not the repetition of boring, routine jobs. All brains need a certain amount of adrenaline to function well. Efficient housekeepers have the right amount to keep them going even if the task is routine. But folks with ADD lack the adrenaline to carry them through these kinds of tasks. They look for exciting or interesting jobs to get the juices flowing. Trust me; emptying the dishwasher and folding laundry does not give the excitement needed to stimulate adrenaline. So, left to herself, the Messie with ADD avoids these jobs like the plague and seeks out some fun activity or project.

Often, people with ADD will comment that they must just be lazy about housework. They state that they can do things they are really interested in perfectly well. They don't realize they need the stimulation of interesting activities to function well.

Most housework is nothing if it is not the repetition of boring, routine jobs.

For this reason, this person often works best under crisis conditions. She will wait until the last minute to prepare for guests, cook dinner, and the like. In school, she typically waited until just before the deadline to begin a paper. The adrenaline high gives the ability to attend to the task. Some would say she is becoming an adrenaline junkie. Still others would say she is just trying to fill an unmet bodily need.

However you look at it, this adrenaline-producing stress is hard on the body and may eventually lead to fatigue of the adrenal glands.

In a way, the mess of the house itself is stimulating. She sees she needs to get the work done. It is a battle, a long-term struggle, a drama she engages in daily. The stress feels comfortable. One of the things the reformed Messie must adjust to is the peacefulness that comes with having the house under control. The lack of struggle takes some getting used to and must be adjusted for.

4. **Impulsiveness.** Irma makes decisions too quickly. She throws something away in a fit of neatness, but a week later she needs it.

I understand the problem. On a train trip from Florida to Indiana, I had a stopover in Memphis, where I decided to clean out my purse. By mistake I kept an empty ticket envelope and threw away the envelope with the rest of my ticket in it. Not until I was on the moving train and the conductor came for my ticket did I realize what I had done.

This happens frequently to impulsive people. Unfortunately, instead of teaching them to be less impulsive, these bad experiences teach them to be hoarders. To keep from throwing away something they may someday need, they throw away nothing. I sure hesitate to discard things from my purse.

It is not just impulsive decisions to throw things away that cause problems for ADD people. When they make a wrong decision as a result of impulsiveness, they learn to not make a decision again. This creates an inertia that leads to procrastination. For instance, an ADD woman may want to attend a workshop, but she never gets around to registering because she doesn't know for sure that she will be able to go. Maybe something else will come up. Maybe she already has an obligation she has forgotten about. Maybe it costs too much. So she waits until she can be sure, and then it's too late.

They sit tight in the comfort of inertia.

Sometimes she doesn't hold back the impulsiveness. In a moment of inattention she does something inappropriate or blurts out something that embarrasses her.

In the back of her mind may lurk the ultimate fear that she will do something really dangerous. A North Carolina photographer and sky diver jumped out of the plane with his fellow sky divers and began to take pictures of them. But when it was time to pull the ripcord he realized he had jumped without his parachute. He was killed on impact. His film survived to show the story. This kind of story frightens people who know they may someday make an impulsive and thoughtless decision of a serious nature because they are distracted. Sometimes this fear keeps them from making any decisions at all. They sit tight in the comfort of inertia.

All of these fears—losing things, forgetting things, not finishing things, doing the wrong thing, doing nothing—cause more work. And because no one can do all this additional work, our families get angry, people put us down, and our self-esteem plummets.

The ADD Struggle

A self-acknowledged Messie from Ohio wrote her observations about the inability to organize. Notice the similarities to the attention deficit disorder we have been discussing.

We Messies are probably victims of a neurological impairment. We cannot take in the larger picture. We are bogged down in details. We do not live on the surface; we are under a heap of impenetrable events, objects, people. We are baffled all the time about which is the next task. To say we struggle valiantly would be an understatement. No one could try more earnestly to make order out of chaos, but it is always just beyond us.

To give a specific example, when I have mustered an incredible amount of courage and have invited guests for dinner, I make lists, shop, and clean well ahead of time. I am a 69-year-old wife with nothing to distract me except one wonderful husband. My situation is the very finest any Messie could ever encounter. Yet, there always come the final moments of preparation when I panic—there is too much! It all needs to be done immediately, if not sooner. One thing at a time will never do it! There is nothing for it but to get on my horse and ride off in all directions at once, NOW. Things fly and get spilled, the tablecloth gets spotted, gravy gets dumped in the sink as I try to strain out the lumps, and so on.

If we were limping along with crutches, people would understand that we have an impairment. But we look and act so normal in most circumstances that no one can comprehend that we are battling just to stay at the same place—getting ahead is out of the question. Yes, it is funny. But if you could feel my heart racing and my breathlessness at the moment when inability lies exposed, with all seriousness I say you would see it is a bit tragic. The best way to describe my state at such times is to say my brain is scrambled, totally disorganized.

We are not a total loss, however. More than an ordinary percentage of us are musicians, artists, and journalists. Our minds are seldom on the ordinary tasks we are doing, but are solving the world's woes. That is why we have to leave everything out in plain view that we do not want to forget.

This is why we have to make endless lists (which we often lose). It is a rather miserable existence but our spirit is unquenchable! Dare I say the world would be a poorer place without us?

No more humiliation needed, so I won't sign my name.

Is There Any Help?

Although some ADD symptoms diminish with age, adults still carry the confusion and fear of those early years. But adults have the advantage of knowing what is going on, which can keep them from kicking themselves around for being lazy, stupid, or disinterested.

The same treatments that apply to children with ADD apply to adults. We cannot diagnose ADD ourselves. Diagnosis must be done by knowledgeable and experienced mental health professionals or physicians. Although ADD is a difficult problem, it can be controlled through medication prescribed by a physician and with careful attention to contributing factors, such as visual problems, diet, and sleep disorders. Educating ourselves about the problem is imperative. Learning to organize and adjust routines to meet special needs will enable folks with ADD to function to maximum potential.

Assess the Mess

1. Do you notice ADD characteristics in your own experience? List them.

   a.

   b.

   c.

2. Were you considered scatterbrained as a child? Write down an incident that stands out in your mind.

3. Have you had a particularly upsetting experience with lack of attention span, distractibility, impulsiveness, or poor social sense as an adult? Explain.

4. How have the characteristics
   a. affected your housekeeping abilities?
   b. influenced your personality and self-esteem?

5. Education is one of the first steps in solving the ADD problem. Do you plan to read further or investigate the possibility of ADD in your life? If so, what exactly do you plan? Will you read a book, perhaps one suggested below?

Bibliography

Amen, Daniel G., M.D. *Healing ADD: The Breakthrough Program that Allows You to See and Heal the Six Types of Attention Deficit Disorder*. New York: G. P. Putnam's Sons, 2001.

Felton, Sandra. *Why Can't I Get Organized?* Miami, FL: Five Smooth Stones Communications, 1998.

Hartmann, Thom. *ADD Success Stories: A Guide to Fulfillment for Families with Attention Deficit Disorder*. Grass Valley, CA: Underwood Books, 1995.

Hollowel, Edward M., M.D., and John J. Ratey, M.D. *Driven to Distraction: Recognizing and Coping with Attention Deficit Disorder from Childhood to Adulthood*. New York: Simon & Schuster, 1994.

Solden, Sari. *Women with Attention Deficit Disorder*. Grass Valley, CA: Underwood Books, 1995.

6

compulsive or just messy?

When does the problem of messiness become the larger problem of compulsion? How can we tell if we're just disorganized or if we have a compulsive character style or a more serious problem called an obsessive-compulsive disorder?

Addictive Personalities?

It is easy to become confused about the differences between addictions, compulsions, phobias, and the like. The words are thrown about with abandon. Professionals tell us there are relationships between these categories.

Notice the similar characteristics of ADD mentioned in the article quoted below, which is written about addictions and compulsions. In an article in *Psychology Today* ("Against All Odds," December 1985) the writer concludes:

Addiction is a mysterious and complex phenomenon. . . . However, certain groups of traits, which are also characteristic of antisocial personalities, are seen in many types of addicts. . . . These include sensation-seeking, a short attention span, hyperactivity, emotional hypersensitivity and inability to delay gratification (absence of impulse control). When combined with a loveless early environment, these qualities often lead people to become compulsive.

We are well acquainted with the problems of addiction to alcohol and other drugs. Although they do not have a physical component like alcohol and drugs, getting hooked on shopping, eating, gambling, and other activities is frequently spoken of as an addiction. Self-help groups have sprung up to address these disorders. In a related field, we are familiar with phobias such as the fear of heights, of flying, and of the outside world. All these addictions, phobias, compulsions, and obsessive behaviors have been widely written about. Although they are not the same, they are similar in that they have to do with losing control. In all the writing about these disorders, however, little has been said about the disorganized lifestyle, although in its extreme it is an officially recognized obsessive-compulsive disorder. It is in the context of these issues that we now consider the problems we face as Messies.

Messiness Ignored

A few parts of the problem we experience have been addressed. For example, procrastination, hoarding, and chronic tardiness get some attention. But little or nothing is written about the lack of neatness, loss of important documents, over-sentimentality that makes everything sacred, or the love of books and magazines that forces us to be priests of the god of knowledge. Many of us are paralyzed in these important facets of life. Whether or not they all meet the criteria of a true disorder, we feel as though we are addicted or caught in some kind of obsessive behavior we cannot control. We try to change, but somehow we can't. Yet few seem to notice our grief.

Messies do not publicize the problem. In a woman's view, her house is an extension of herself. From our earliest days we associated the house with our mothers and what they provided. Women are nest builders. It is said that even animals do not foul their own nests. But Messies do. This says ugly things to a woman about herself. So like everything else, Messies hide this secret in the closet and, with everything else, they leave it there.

Obsessive-Compulsive Disorder

Not everyone who is messy has an obsessive-compulsive disorder. Dr. Harvey Milkman, professor of psychology at Metropolitan State College in Denver, gives some guidelines to determine whether you may be approaching a serious problem with compulsion.

1. Denial. Does your family complain about the house and your part in it? Do you deny that you have a problem? (Does the statement, "Something has got to be done about this place! This is driving me crazy!" sound familiar?)
2. Compulsion. You have tried to change but you can't. You want to be neat, stop procrastinating, and stop saving, but it's somehow beyond your power.
3. Loss of Control. You are more and more drawn to the behavior. You do not have the time, energy, or will to stop.
4. Progression. Life has gotten less and less satisfying. You feel you cannot go out because you have work to do at the house. You can't invite others over without working yourself to death to get ready or letting the housework go and being embarrassed. More and more you are losing things and forgetting appointments.
5. Withdrawal. When you try to change, you find that you have altered patterns of sleep, eating, or social interaction.

> Compulsive people—both messy and neat—are trying to gain control of a world that seems to be very much out of control.

If you try to get rid of things or challenge your perfectionism, you become depressed or upset. It frightens you to think of doing things differently.

If you answered yes to questions in three or more of these areas, Dr. Milkman says you are on the road to a behavioral addiction, or you are already there. People are drawn into these addictive types of behavior to enhance their own coping devices. We have all seen pictures of the homey farmhouse approach to decorating. Pots and pans hang from the rafters. Bric-a-brac adorns the shelves. Messies personify the homey approach run amuck. We fill spaces long after reaching the stylish point. We end up with junk. People hardly recognize that we were trying for the homey look. We have all of our papers and memorabilia—somewhere—and someday we will look at them, if we stumble across them before we die. In short, Messies take good, normal activities and seriously overdo them.

normal activity	becomes	compulsive activity
frugality		saving things unnecessarily
sentimentality		obsessive hoarding of items from the past
foresight		keeping every scrap "just in case"
caution		paralysis from fear of making mistakes

Things Get Complicated

Frequently we get so caught up in these activities that we fail to notice the toll they take. When people write to me about their struggles, they often mention drowning, or they draw a picture of themselves drowning in clutter. A drowning person is caught in something deadly. Drowning is the ultimate lack of control.

Not everyone who drinks becomes an alcoholic. Not everyone who gambles gets hooked on it. Not everyone who diets becomes bulimic or anorexic. Not everyone who saves, clutters, or procrastinates becomes seriously embroiled in the problem. Why do some fall into that category we loosely call addiction to clutter? The answer is far from complete, but some facts are known.

Low self-esteem is said to be the cornerstone of addiction. The causes of low self-esteem relate mainly to the development of a faulty self-image in childhood, which can be caused by a number of things. We know there is an abnormally high incidence of sexual trauma in the background of women with addiction problems. Many have unhappy childhoods. Some studies indicate that adult children of alcoholics are more prone to addictive problems of all types. In *Guide to Recovery: A Book for Adult Children of Alcoholics*, Herbert L. Gravitz and Julie D. Bowden, founding members of the National Association for Children of Alcoholics, write, "Children of alcoholics are at maximum risk of becoming alcoholics themselves or developing other addictive behavior."

As mentioned earlier, those with ADD are more prone to compulsion. Until recently there has been little research on the personalities, motivations, or psychological aspects of the lives of compulsive Messies.

Stanton Peele, author of *Love and Addiction* and *The Meaning of Addiction*, says, "A person will be predisposed to addiction to the extent that he cannot establish a meaningful relationship to his environment as a whole, and thus cannot develop a fully elaborated life. In this case, he will be susceptible to a mindless absorption in something external to himself."

Compulsive people—both messy and neat—are trying to gain control of a world that seems to be very much out of control. This feeling of control brings comfort, which is a precious commodity in a stressful world. Always present, however, is the overriding fear of losing control.

Of course, there are other factors at work as well. Genetics, peer pressure, and cultural influences all play a part in whether or not a person becomes compulsive. Obsessive-compulsive disorders of various kinds affect about six million Americans. Gender plays a part as well. For example, there are more female bulimics and anorexics than male. There are more male compulsive gamblers than female.

Knowing our intrinsic value tempers our compulsion to prove who we are through extreme behavior.

Men generally explain their behavior in terms of choices. They keep things they want. Women explain their behavior in terms of feelings. They keep things they love. Men tend to become Messies for practical reasons. They keep junk cars in the yard to use for parts that are hard to find. Women, on the other hand, become Messies for personal reasons. They feel an attachment to their belongings. They love their books, their sewing, and the like. They keep them to sustain personal satisfaction.

Whatever the reason we got into this situation, it is not working out for us now. We can't get out of the mess (so to speak) we are in. Where can a person find the change she is looking for? Whether or not you are a truly compulsive Messie, you will find help in following some of these paths to recovery:

1. **Admit the problem.** This is perhaps the hardest part. Some Messies can hardly face the idea of giving up the lifestyle that has been so much a part of their lives.

2. **Get help.** Join groups that address the basic self-esteem problem or join a Messies Anonymous group geared toward motivation and education. Perhaps therapy with someone familiar with compulsive problems will get you started on the road to recovery. Promising new medications are available to treat some types of obsessive-compulsive disorders.

In *The Compulsive Woman*, Sandra LeSourd gives eighty pages of references of help for compulsive people, including the spiritual dimension, where she found much of her help. In the end, however, we are responsible to make sure we get the help we need. "It takes time, effort, and faith to mature out of an addictive disposition. . . . Therapy or no, the ultimate responsibility is still our own" (*Love and Addiction*, Stanton Peele).

3. **Get a new perspective.** Many people, both Cleanies and Messies, find that a spiritual dimension in their lives helps moderate their extremes. A good friend of mine, a compulsive Cleanie, noticed that she became less compulsive about neatness as she matured as a believer. The fruit of the Spirit, says the apostle Paul, is temperance. Temperance is moderation in action, thought, or feeling. Those who have God's Spirit have his help in modifying the drive to save, leave things out, and overcrowd the calendar. A personal relationship with God also gives us a sense of who we are and why we were created. Knowing our intrinsic value tempers our compulsion to prove who we are through extreme behavior.

Those who follow the directives found in the Bible will pay special attention to the admonition to lay aside the weights that so easily beset us and hinder us from running the race of life that God has set before us. For us, clutter is one of those weights we want to lay aside so we will be free to run well.

4. **Begin new behavior.** The new behavior will not be as comforting as the old, nor as self-destructive. In *Hope: New Choices and Recovery Strategies for Adult Children of Alcoholics*, Emily Marlin writes, "It is important to note that it's not unusual to feel a sense of loss after giving up an addiction—even when abstinence is desperately wanted." She speaks of addiction in terms of alcohol addiction, but her insights apply to others as well, including messiness. "Giving up the alcohol means the alcoholic also has to give up a certain lifestyle that, though destructive, meets some of his or her needs."

Recovering from messiness is not like overcoming any other problem because messiness involves so much of what we must do every day. When arising, the Messie must make the bed, not walk away from it as before. After breakfast, she must clear the table and take care of the dishes, not pile them on the counter or leave them on the table. When the mail comes, she has to handle it immediately instead of putting it in a pile. In addition to establishing "doing" habits to replace "neglecting" habits, the recovering Messie is faced with the years of neglect gathered in every corner of the house. When a person gives up smoking or drinking, she is faced with stopping and staying stopped. When a person gives up messiness, she is faced with starting and continuing a number of things.

Life is a marathon, not a sprint.

Recovering from messiness is also different from smoking and drinking in that it requires moderation, not abstinence. Moderation is hard for compulsive people. Abstinence is easier. A reforming Messie must decide what to keep and what to get rid of. She can't get rid of everything. Making those decisions is very difficult. Recovering from messiness may be compared to recovering from overeating. A person must eat something. The trick is to make wise choices about what to eat and to eat moderately.

On the whole, Messies are not naturally moderate. They overdo in what they keep, and they overdo in their activities. One of the problems a recovering Messie will face is the desire to overdo in the other direction and get the house under too much control. Messies who catch the vision of the new way of life want it right away. More than one Messie has exhausted herself by plunging headlong into changing the house. With a jaded eye she looks back over her short experience of trying to change and assures herself that she has proven that it does not work. She can never change. She tried and failed. What she did was exchange one compulsion for another. No wonder it didn't work. A moderate, sustained approach works best. As I frequently remind Messies, life is a marathon, not a sprint. A person may slip and return to her old habits. Studies have shown that this does not mean all is lost. When she returns to the recovery program, she is stronger than when she first started and can continue with hope for success.

Much is being written about compulsive behavior. We are learning more and more. Help is available from many sources. The compulsion to messiness is an area in which much work needs to be done. We do not need to wait for the final results before we get help for ourselves, however. Many people have overcome messiness already. If more powerful techniques arise, wonderful. But in the meantime we can be free.

Slow but Sure

The motto of *The Organizer Lady* daily newsletter found on the online support group page of www.messies.com is "The secret to success is making very small, yet very consistent, changes." Members of online groups of www.messies.com often encourage each other to take "baby steps." This phrase, which came from the movie *What about Bob?*, encourages us to make moderate, consistent changes in the direction of orderliness.

The best way to do this is to establish a new *routine*, that ugliest of all words in the Messie vocabulary. A little at a time, we start doing things differently. We set up the house at night in preparation for the morning. We fully dress first thing instead of sitting around in nightclothes. We empty the dishwasher as soon as possible after the dishes are washed, so we are not forced to put dirties in the sink or on the counter. We remove clothes from the dryer as soon as they are finished, fold them, and put them away in one continuous movement. We engage the family in a meaningful team effort to get things done. And on it goes, building a new life a little at a time.

New patterns of doing things, new thought habits, new ways of feeling must come slowly if they are to be maintained. Often it takes repeated reminders before these foreign behaviors become a part of our lives. It takes longer still before they become automatic. Then one day we wake up and find we have been brainwashed by the repeated reminders and admonitions of our reading, our friends online, our group meetings. We kept moving forward even when we had set-backs. We did not notice we were making progress. But by challenging our old behaviors, thoughts, and feelings, we have loosened their hold on us.

To our surprise, one day we find our lives are different. We have less stress and feel less struggle in our lives. We can open the front door to the neighbor instead of stepping out on the porch, closing the door behind us. We can even consider asking people over to the house if we can overcome the fear built up over so many years. We no longer dread coming home. It is now a haven, not another work area. We come into the bedroom and are startled to see the bed is made. We did it automatically.

Life is good. Things are not hopeless. We are not at the mercy of instincts and inbred behaviors. We can make deliberate choices. If we make them consistently by an act of our will, eventually those choices will make us. Here I offer you good news. Very, very good news.

Assess the Mess

1. Look at the five signs of obsessive-compulsive behavior in Dr. Milkman's checklist. Do you recognize any of these as part of your problem? Which one(s)?

   a.
   b.
   c.

2. If you recognize compulsive behavior in yourself and think you might profit from outside help, what steps will you take?

   a. Start or join a Messies Anonymous self-help group, join an online support group at www.messies.com, or subscribe to *The Organizer Lady* daily reminder newsletter offered on that site.

b. Start therapy with a professional skilled in treating compulsions. If you choose this option, look for a psychiatrist (or someone associated with a psychiatrist) so that medication can be prescribed if necessary.

3. Do you notice any compulsive tendencies in any areas other than housekeeping (eating, gambling, drinking, relationships, and so on)? Explain.

7

parenting the child within

Ann loved her father. No one treated her any better than he did—when he was sober. But as Ann grew older, her father's sober times grew shorter. By the time she entered high school, her father's job got all his sober moments. For a long time Ann believed that if she could be a better daughter her dad would come home instead of getting drunk. Her efforts to please him by being neat led Ann to borderline compulsive behavior. Whatever she did, she did perfectly. She didn't just clean closets; she arranged them like a display window. Soon Ann got to the point where she didn't have time to put anything where it belonged because it took too long to arrange it perfectly. As a result, her bedroom became piled with clothes, shoes, and accessories she didn't put away because doing so would destroy the order in her closet. Ann's efforts to control her father by controlling her own behavior caused her to lose control of everything. She became a slave to her own unrealistic demands.

The chapter on addiction mentions that adult children of alcoholics are at maximum risk of developing addictive behavior. It may be true, therefore, that people who are powerless to organize their lives were raised in homes made dysfunctional by alcoholism, divorce, mental illness, depression, violence, or abuse.

This chapter shows how people learn to relate to disorganization in childhood. It will be of special interest to those who know, or vaguely suspect, that the homes in which they were raised were dysfunctional.

Messies frequently mention to me that they are members of a self-help group other than Messies Anonymous. As mentioned earlier, it is not unusual for people to be dealing with more than one problem area at a time, since addictions and compulsions commonly travel in groups.

If a dysfunctional childhood is at the core of your disorganization, success in changing will come about only by facing and resolving those core issues. One of the first things we need to do is clean out the old ways of thinking and feeling that cause us to act in such self-destructive ways. We need to make space for new thinking, which will lead us to the order, beauty, and peace we seek.

In the early 1980s, a group of people who had been raised in dysfunctional families, usually alcoholic families, began recognizing the issues they were dealing with as a group. Organizations of adult children of alcoholics were formed and many books were written in an effort to help this newly emerging group overcome the negative effects of their childhood experiences.

Looking at Characteristics

Some of the general characteristics of adult children of alcoholics correspond with a Messie's struggles in adult life. In some people they are related. In others, they may simply act as an informative parallel.

1. **Control.** Control is the one word that most characterizes the interactions of adult children of alcoholics. While it applies

to other aspects of life, it also applies to housekeeping. Paradoxically, a messy house is frequently the result of a Messie's effort to stay in control of her life. She has gathered and stored more than necessary so she will always have what she needs. Much of it is sitting out for easy access.

A child whose needs have been chronically ignored because of the family's primary obligation to alcohol learns to subjugate and minimize her own needs.

One reason that "how to" approaches to cleaning do not work for many people is that they do not address the fear of being out of control. Emily Marlin speaks of this fear in her book *Hope: New Choices and Recovery Strategies for Adult Children of Alcoholics*: "The conflict, confusion, and chaos in the alcoholic home made it seem necessary for us to try to exert control over ourselves and others, simply in order to survive. We had to stay in control in spite of, and because of, the terrible fear that any minute everything could spin out of control."

Many people do not realize that hoarding things and keeping them in view is an attempt at control.

2. Overresponsible and Underresponsible. When the adults in a family are dysfunctional, a child will often step in to meet the needs of the family. She tries to carry the load the adults in the family have dropped. Sometimes this works, and the child, by becoming an "adult," is able to meet with some success in helping the family, albeit at the expense of her own childhood. I believe this is one reason many Messies feel the need to be the "mother of the world." As children, they put aside their own needs to meet the needs of others. As adults, that is all they know how to do. Many sincere and responsible adults continue in this destructive role forced on them in childhood.

This mother-of-the-world feeling is one reason some Messies cram their lives so full of altruistic activities, such as Boy Scouts, church work, jobs in the healing or helping professions, and commitment to causes and charities. These are worthy activities when balanced with other aspects of life, but the person who reacts in a mechanical way to meeting needs goes to an extreme that is self-destructive.

In another way, however, these Messies may be under-responsible. Years of struggling against a power larger than themselves, and losing, has taught them that some things are beyond their control. They feel defeated. Disorderliness, for many, is one of the overwhelming forces they feel unable to control.

There are two other possibilities when considering the relationship to disorder of those from a dysfunctional background. Even though their childhood houses may have been neat, they have lived in personal chaos for so long that they have learned to tolerate a great deal more mess than one would guess possible. Indeed, some may prefer the stimulation of chaos, fearing that life in a neat and orderly house would be boring.

The second thought to consider is that the house is a reflection of the chaos that still exists within the heart of the Messie with a chaotic background. Clutter in the home will not dissipate until the clutter in the heart, which it reflects, is cleaned up.

Many people who have a dysfunctional background are able to control the disorder in their lives. As a matter of fact, extreme neatness is one of the comforts many such children find in a chaotic world. While Mom and Dad fought and threw things around, their children found comfort in neatly folded underwear and meticulously aligned hangers in the closet. As stated earlier, extreme neatness and extreme messiness are different ends of the same continuum. Some go one way and some go another in response to the stress in their lives.

Writing to me about the help she found in my previous books, a Messie shared the following thoughts. They illustrate how chaos passes from one generation to another and how one child reacted to that chaos with her own version of control.

As a child, I was often told by my mother that I was a slob. My mother once found termites on the windowsills and launched into a half-hour tirade that it was all because I ate cookies in the living room. "I need order! I hate dirt!" she would often say. What wasn't mentioned was that she was chronically depressed and an alcoholic. This was a result of a horrible childhood, but it was never brought up. Denial and self-delusion lived in our house with us. At the age of sixteen I caught my first glimmer of the real truth. Mom was sleeping, and I went searching the kitchen cabinets for something to eat. We had always had a problem with tiny bugs in our kitchen, but Mom would blame it on the fact that we used oil heat "and everyone knows grease attracts bugs." On the top shelf of the cabinet over the stove was a pile of two-year-old spaghetti boxes, flour bags, sugar bags (none of them sealed), and of course, lots of happy, busy bugs. It finally dawned on me that I wasn't the only "slob" in the house, and from that time on I put myself in charge of keeping the cabinets in order.

3. **Ignoring their own needs and feelings.** One of the emphases throughout this book is how to tune in to our own needs. This has a much broader application than housekeeping, of course, but our goal is to see how living in a dysfunctional family may create problems in the housekeeping area. We create much of the dysfunctional living in our homes because we do not care enough about our own need for beauty, our personal tastes, or our need to have the proper equipment. A child whose needs have been chronically ignored because of the family's primary obligation to alcohol learns to subjugate and minimize her own needs.

Perhaps, awakening to the concept of self-care, the Messie decides to be especially kind to herself. But she can't really figure out how to go about doing that. "One of the saddest symptoms of codependency is our inability to take care of ourselves," write John and Linda Friel in *An Adult Child's Guide to What Is "Normal"* ([Deerfield Beach, FL: Health Communications, 1990], 85).

Alcohol-involved family members may be doing the best they can to meet the child's needs, but their primary commitment is to the alcohol. This lack of attention eventually leads to the child's low self-esteem, the backbone of addictive and compulsive behavior. The child begins to believe that her needs are not being met because she is not important. Eventually she feels guilty about expressing her own needs because she believes she is imposing on others.

This failure to recognize or express her own needs may lead the Messie to try to do without, to deny herself the things average successful housekeepers take for granted. The Messie with this background may feel uncomfortable asking for her family's help with chores or spending family money on the house. Enough self-denial may eventually frustrate the Messie to the point where she explodes, demands help in a tantrum (though she is not quite sure what kind of help she needs), feels guilty about her behavior, and returns to the chronic denial of her needs until the frustration explodes again.

In a similar way, the child in a dysfunctional home learns to subjugate and ignore her own emotions. She is afraid of anger because she remembers the destruction it caused in her home. She was told that nothing was wrong when she knew something was very wrong. She was expected to have patience and understanding far beyond her years, and to control confusion and impatience, she learned to suppress her emotions. They just caused trouble. To escape the grim realities of home and to avoid dealing with emotions, she filled her life with activities. Today she still packs her calendar full, partly out of habit and partly to keep the feelings in abeyance.

This avoidance of emotion carries into her adult life in ways that may not be apparent on the surface. For instance, the Messie who doesn't know what she prefers cannot settle on any particular decorating style. Nothing really excites her. This may be why practicality, not beauty, plays such a strong role in some Messies' thinking. Beauty involves emotion and feeling, practicality doesn't.

When I have a cold, I tend to eat more. Because my sense of taste is lessened, I keep eating to find something that satisfies me. In a similar way, the inability to feel may be part of what propels Messies to be excessive collectors. They continually

The inability to feel may be part of what propels Messies to be excessive collectors. They continually hope to find something that will stimulate the feelings they are missing.

hope to find something that will stimulate the feelings they are missing.

There are other characteristics that are often cited when discussing this problem. Some are characteristics that will definitely lead to a cluttered house: difficulty following projects through to the end, looking for immediate as opposed to deferred gratification, poor time and priority management. And, of course, there is the obvious relationship: a lifestyle that is chaotic in relationships or career areas tends to throw living conditions into chaos as well. Divorce, monetary needs, forced moves, or whatever behavior emanates from a life poorly lived makes it hard to keep things in order. In this case, as in others, the house is a symptom urging us to find the cause and seek health in that area of our lives.

The Real Cause of Messiness

You may want to know which of the many causes of messiness I have suggested is the real one. Is it ADD? Is it compulsive behavior? Is it being brought up in a dysfunctional home? The truth is, these things tend to run together. One or all may contribute to the problem of messiness. It is unlikely that all of the factors mentioned apply to you. And some things significant to you may not be covered. The causes I have given are a starting point to examine your own situation and decide how to get help for yourself. In the end, you are responsible for your own recovery.

"It is the spirit in a man, the breath of the Almighty, that gives him understanding" (Job 32:8). Having been enlightened, you are now the parent who must raise the confused child within you who is trying to live an adult life without the necessary tools. Go gently. Be kind to yourself. Be as wise as possible. And God bless you.

Assess the Mess

1. Was there a dysfunction in the home you grew up in that may be affecting your life today? What dysfunction? Explain.

2. Does your messiness give you a feeling of control? If so, how?

3. Do you relate to your housekeeping in an overly responsible way? Are you perfectionistic in some aspects of housekeeping? Explain.

4. How do you feel about being irresponsible? Do you relate it to a feeling of powerlessness learned in childhood?

5. What steps will you take to resolve those issues? You may want to read books about growing up in a dysfunctional home. You may wish to join an existing Messies Anonymous group or start one in your area. For more information, see Appendix B.

8

fatigue

Let's say clearly what is abundantly obvious but few people actually come right out and say when they talk about organizing. If you are sick, or in pain, or suffering from some kind of low-grade health problem, all this talk about how to organize the house, how to overcome the tendency to clutter, or whatever, just isn't going to work for you. If you can't get your body to cooperate, what good is knowing what to do?

Out of concern for those who are in this condition and know it and those who are in this condition and don't yet realize what is wrong, this situation needs to be addressed.

My special concern is that there are some women who are reading this book with a great deal of emotional commitment, personal resolve, and frank desperation, and it's just not happening for them because their primary problem has not yet been touched on. They are just not functioning well physically. They can't figure out what is wrong. In order to make sense of why they are not functioning, they say they are lazy, would rather read, have more important interests than housework, or whatever makes sense to them to explain why they are not correcting a problem that has been a long-term distress. It may be that the problem is so low-grade and has been with them for so long they don't realize the lack of energy they experience is not natural.

Doctors report that fatigue is one of the most common complaints they encounter. Its cause is hard to diagnose. It may be caused by a number of underlying disorders. The following information is readily available with minimal research. I mention these more common problems to focus you on your health, particularly how health-related fatigue, forgetfulness, and the like impacts your organizational skills.

Over the years various conditions that relate to fatigue, primarily in women, have enjoyed their day in the sun. Early in my memory I recall that fatigue was blamed on what was called "iron-poor blood." Later low blood sugar, low thyroid function, and chronic fatigue syndrome marched across the stage of popular thinking. Each of these should be considered in answering the question women have asked through the years, "Why am I so tired?" The problem is to find out which of the many possibilities apply to you and your condition.

Only a doctor can make a diagnosis and prescribe a remedy, but your health will improve as you participate. Only as you inform yourself will you be able to make the choices that are part of your responsibility in gaining the health you need to live the life you want.

Low Adrenal Function

Messies live with a lot of stress because the clutter, the personal and family stress caused by the mess, and the idea that life is out of control put us under tremendous pressure. All of this stress stimulates our adrenal glands to overproduce adrenaline to cope. Our adrenal glands become fatigued and eventually falter. We weren't built to live like this. What was supposed to be there for energy support is not there any longer.

The person who feels groggy in the morning, has trouble dragging herself out of bed, has difficulty falling asleep, has low sex interest, and is tired all the time may have adrenal glands that are not functioning. Foggy thinking, insomnia, hypoglycemia, depression, poor memory, headaches, cravings for sweets, and use of caffeine for stimulation are further evidence of adrenal dysfunction.

You can see how the tiredness, foggy thinking, and poor memory combined with the other symptoms would make organizing a chore.

Low Thyroid Function (or Hypothyroidism)

Over fourteen million Americans have hypothyroidism, seven times as many women as men. Depression, weight gain, and poor concentration are all part of the picture. The symptoms of low thyroid function that may interfere with what we are trying to accomplish in our houses and lives are feeling sluggish, run down, slow, and uninterested in daily activities. Diagnosing thyroid problems is tricky, even with improved tests available. Sometimes the tests show the person falls within the average range of thyroid function, but their symptoms improve when they are treated with medication to increase the thyroid hormone in their system to the upper average range.

Chronic Fatigue Syndrome and Fibromyalgia

There is a great deal of disagreement in the medical field about the place of these diagnoses, although they are becoming more accepted. Chronic fatigue syndrome (CFS) is characterized by serious fatigue and includes other symptoms, such as intermittent joint pain and painful lymph nodes. It has been related to the Epstein-Barr virus.

Fibromyalgia is thought by some to be related to CFS. It is characterized by muscle aches and stiffness, sleeplessness, and fatigue. The causes are not clear. Some who have been diagnosed with fibromyalgia complain of intermittent episodes of confusion or disorientation, which they call among themselves a "fibrofog." This fogginess, along with the pain and fatigue, greatly interferes with their ability to get and keep the house organized.

Anemia

Called "iron-poor blood" by early advertisers of remedies, anemia is a shortage of red blood cells usually caused by iron deficiency. It affects up to 40 percent of premenopausal women. A person who lacks red blood cells becomes generally tired and lethargic. In most cases, it is reasonably easy to diagnose and treat through diet and supplementation of iron. However, just taking iron may not be the total answer because sometimes there are interferences with absorption that need to be addressed.

Hypoglycemia

Hypoglycemia is a rare condition related to serious diseases and is not related to our topic. However, another form called reactive hypoglycemia has symptoms similar to those that occur when a diabetic takes an overdose of insulin. These are rapid heartbeat, sweating, headache, and fatigue that occur after eating. Neither diagnosis nor treatment is well understood, but some people who have these symptoms improve by lowering their carbohydrate intake, eating more protein, and taking frequent small meals rather than three large ones.

Problems with Pain

Nobody feels like moving when it hurts. Pain wears you out more quickly than almost anything. Diseases that cause pain are definitely going to interfere with getting things done. Whatever the cause of the pain (do we really need to name them all?), you need to do a couple of things. First, get adequate medical intervention to treat the cause and manage the pain. Once you have attended to that, you need to adjust your circumstances to deal with your situation. That may mean asking for or hiring additional help, simplifying your life, changing your way of doing things, and adapting your surroundings to meet your needs.

Physical Limitations

If you break your leg or arm, you will have to curtail your work temporarily. I mention this obvious fact because some women I know try to keep going in spite of it all. Don't. You need to make adjustments.

While some injuries cause temporary problems, some women live with long-term physical limitations that affect their ability to function. My observation has been that those with these kinds of limitations often have to become organized in order to get along in the face of their handicap.

One of my first clues that I did not have any really good excuse for continuing my own messiness was when I visited in the neat-as-a-pin home of a friend with very serious cerebral palsy. Though she walked with great difficulty and had trouble controlling the rest of her body, she kept house for herself and her husband without outside help.

I had one of those moments when a bell went off in my head. *What handicap am I not overcoming?* I asked myself. *And why not?*

A blind friend of mine told me she was very messy until she became blind. Before she lost her sight, the police were called to the house for a robbery. They thought her room had been vandalized. She didn't tell them that the condition of her room was the way she had left it. The thieves had probably become discouraged when they looked in and left her room alone. I guess there are some advantages to being messy. Later when she lost her sight, she had to change her messy ways in order to function.

My final example is my own mother who is eighty-eight and in a wheelchair because of osteoporosis. She lives alone with part-time help, and her house is immaculate. She has lived in small apartments and large houses, worked outside the home and stayed home, had plenty of money and less than enough. Through all the ups and downs of her long life, one thing has remained constant: her living quarters have never been anything but neat and tidy.

I don't want to downplay the difficulties involved. Sometimes a physical limitation is the catalyst that forces folks into an organized lifestyle. Sometimes counseling or occupational training is part of the improvement

But, strange as it seems, in my experience physical limitations (within certain boundaries, of course) don't seem to be an overriding impediment to orderliness if the person has an orderly mind-set. These folks give hope to those who have physical limitations and challenge those of us who don't struggle with the burden of additional physical hindrances. If they can do it, surely we can.

Other Interferences

A myriad of physical factors may be causing you problems with getting your act together. I have touched on only some of the most obvious. Don't ignore symptoms including tiredness, forgetfulness, or a feeling of confusion. Do your best to find out the cause of whatever symptoms you experience and do your best to find the solutions you need.

One of these factors may be a sleep disorder such as apnea, which affects as many as twelve million Americans. Fifty million Americans suffer from allergies (both food and airborne), fatigue being one of the symptoms, along with congestion and a runny nose. In addition, nutritional deficiencies, obesity, chronic severe headaches, onset of serious diseases, some medications, or other obscure factors that have not even been discovered as yet may be what is wearing you out and tripping you up in your housekeeping.

An experience of mine spotlights how obscure some of these reasons can be. At one time I was experiencing serious fatigue. It was true that I was leading a busy life, teaching full time, taking care of my family, and the like. But whereas I had previously been able to function when I got home in the afternoon, now I was hardly able to do anything. I did little or no work around the house; I went to bed very early. Nothing helped.

I went to my doctor about the problem. He took a blood test, which came back normal. He then told me I must be depressed and wrote a prescription for an antidepressant. I had experienced depression many years before and would have been grateful for medication if I needed it now. Actually, I would have snatched it up. But I really didn't think that was the problem.

So I went to another doctor who did the same thing with the same result and offered me another prescription for depression. Depression is a common cause of fatigue and, I guess, is the first thing on the doctor's list of causes if the blood tests are normal. Since they didn't go any further in their diagnosis and treatment, I was still without help for my problem.

You need to know that for many years I had enjoyed a vegetarian diet, excluding meat of any kind, including fish. As it happened, just about the time I was going to the doctor, I made a change in my eating habits and began including meat in my diet. To my surprise, my fatigue disappeared immediately. When I told the doctor what had happened, his response was "You're kidding!"

The blood test had reflected no problem. He never knew the reason. I never knew the reason. I had just stumbled on the solution. Maybe I had not managed my diet properly. You and I can guess that maybe it had to do with lack of adequate protein. Who knows? But whatever the cause, eating meat solved the problem.

The point is, there are lots of reasons for the fatigue that interferes with our lives and our ability to keep our houses organized. We need to do our best to find and solve them. Often we are both the first and last line of defense when it comes to our health.

Obviously, medical problems should not be treated just so we can get the house in order. But neither should we overlook the fact that often symptoms come to the surface exactly at the point we are discussing, the messiness of the house. The woman who ignores clues from her body may begin to pay attention to them when she can no longer keep the house neat. Now her condition gets her attention! Now she feels she ought to get help!

9

depression

Let's face it. Living in a cluttered house is enough to depress anybody. That is easy to understand. But sometimes the house is not the primary cause of the depression. The cause and effect are reversed. The depression has so weakened the organizational ability of the depressed person that the condition of the house begins to deteriorate. Often these two factors work in tandem. The depressed person isn't up to tackling the house. The house gets worse, contributing to more depression. The situation spirals downward until the condition of the house is so bad that the thought of tackling the mess would buckle the resolve of a person with a vigorous mental outlook.

The Messie, already weakened by her frame of mind, then has one of two choices. She can pluckily call upon herself to begin to turn the situation around, or she can give up entirely. By reading this book, you indicate that you are still willing to try.

Depression Observed

"According to recent research, about 3 percent of Americans—some 19 million—suffer from chronic depressions," writes Andrew Soloman in *The Noonday Demon: An Atlas of Depression* ([New York: Scribner, 2001], 25). The problem is growing. About 10 percent of the population will experience a major depression sometime in their lives. About 50 percent will experience some symptoms of depression. Most will not receive appropriate treatment. The cost to society in money, time, and personal tragedy is astronomical.

When a person who is only an expert on organization takes it upon herself to write about a serious subject such as depression, there is always the danger that the subject will be misrepresented. However, because it is spoken of so often by those who come together for mutual help with messiness, I would be remiss if I did not address it in the context of the problem of disorganization.

The connection is clear. According to Richard O'Connor in his book *Active Treatment of Depression*, "Procrastination is one of the principle behavioral manifestations of depression" (140). Clutter is accumulation caused by many unmade decisions, many unhandled small tasks. Putting off handling the daily mail, unloading the dishwasher, making the bed, hanging up clothes, folding laundry, or other regular activities that daily living presents leads rapidly to stuff sitting around waiting for attention.

Mild depression (if any depression can truly be called mild) is a gradual, sometimes permanent thing. The danger is that the one who suffers with it will become so accustomed to it that it will begin to feel normal. It comes in like fog and gradually takes the color out of life. Muscles weaken. Ordinary actions seem to require more effort than they are worth. The person feels tired and bored. Sometimes the person can keep slogging through the mire of daily activities and getting things done. Occasionally depressed persons become even more detail- and neatness-oriented. But those of us who are predisposed to disorder often find the house reflects our malaise almost immediately.

Major depression, which is a serious, debilitating, major illness, is way beyond the scope of this discussion, as are all the major illnesses that may, as a side effect, impact the house. Those who experience serious depression need to educate themselves further and seek medical intervention quickly.

Double depression is when a person who is experiencing chronic, low-grade depression has occasional periodic bouts of serious depression and then returns to the chronic depression that is the state of her daily life.

What Causes Depression

There are two ways of looking at mild depression. Often it is the result of unconscious negative thought patterns. Sometimes it is caused by some known reason. In other cases, no cause can be pinpointed. If you feel bad for no reason, you are depressed. If you feel bad for a reason, you are also depressed. Probably the best way out of this depression is to tackle the reasons for the depression.

The reasons for depression are many. Sustained stress from the fact that the house is out of control is enough to get any sane person down. Maybe you can't seem to get organized no matter how hard you try, and your family is suffering from the disorganized way of life. Your marriage is faltering. You have worn yourself out. You have lost hope and, with it, motivation.

Suppose someone were to come into your house, give you a warm hug and a cup of tea, and wave a magic wand creating a neat, organized, and attractive place. If you were given the ability to maintain it easily, would your problems be pretty much solved? If so, then solving the house problem is probably where you should focus your energy.

Sometimes you are depressed by something that has nothing to do with the house but reflects on it. Perhaps you have lost someone dear to you. The light of your life has dimmed.

Depression is an attempt not to feel. In this condition, among other things, keeping house seems pointless. For what? For whom?

At other times, those who have suffered loss will gather their belongings around them for comfort. It is not uncommon to find that a tendency to hoard starts when a person begins to realize the uncertainty of life. Gathering and keeping things comforts them and, perhaps more importantly, distracts them from their grief.

Whatever the reasons for depression, they need to be addressed. Humans are wonderfully made and can sometimes improve with the help of God and support from loving friends and family. By drawing on the depths of strength in themselves and taking an active role in solving the problem, such as the condition of the house, they move out of the slough of despondency.

But sometimes, the thing proves to be too strong for self-help alone. Expert help is needed in addition to the help of God, others who love us, and our best effort. Mild depression, and certainly major depression, should never be taken lightly, neglected, or allowed to go too long without remedy. The more quickly it is reversed, the better.

A common approach is to say that depression is just anger turned inward or that it is simply caused by a low level of serotonin. It is easy to inappropriately simplify any problem. While there may be aspects of truth to these ideas, depression is much more complex than that and deserves appropriate and expert treatment.

Relation to Other Problems

Depression is sometimes associated with other disorders. How they relate is not always understood. O'Connor suggests that those who are depressed may use the symptoms of other disorders to ward off and distract from the pain they are feeling.

He states that people with ADHD (attention deficit disorder with hyperactivity) are at high risk for depression. "Some adult manifestations of ADHD can be considered skills of depression because they come to serve a definite purpose. Impulsivity and distractibility, for instance, can keep an individual busy for a lifetime while very little is accomplished in the long run." He points out another way ADHD can work to the benefit of the depressed person when he says, "The ability to hyperfocus can help us rescue the failed project at the last possible moment, supporting procrastination and adrenaline addiction" (58).

The link between obsessive-compulsive disorder and depression is strong but is not well understood. Again O'Connor comments on the connection when he says, "Many patients with depression use obsessive-compulsive defenses without meeting the criteria for OCD. They can be behavior patterns that pass the time and distract from the pain of depression or ritual that we use to propitiate the gods of depression. Cleanliness and messiness are areas of life where many people enact their depression" (56).

What to Do about Depression

For our purposes, several things can be suggested for someone whose depression leads to messiness and a life out of control.

Develop a morning routine. Set up a few steps for yourself in the morning. Set your alarm. Shower, brush your teeth, and fix your hair. A little makeup is a good idea too. Get fully dressed even if you don't plan to go out. Make the bed immediately upon rising and put on real shoes (house slippers won't do), so you won't be so tempted to go back to bed. Focusing on personal behavior is essential to beginning to improve.

If you don't have a pet, you might want to get one. Cats or dogs will insist you get up and start your routine of feeding, walking, or letting them out. They offer unconditional love. Warning: Messies often have too many cats, dogs, or the like. They cause problems with accidents, reproducing, smelling, and generally messing up the house. Their problems just add to your depression. Don't overdo it. If you have already collected too many beloved pets, start considering how you can begin to place them elsewhere.

Seek an organizing plan for the house. Try to do a little every day, no matter how small. Use the Mount Vernon Method for organizing on a deeper level. For a quick, emergency, surface cleanup, use the Mount Vesuvius Method. Both are described in *The Messies Manual* and on the www.messies .com page called "How to Begin."

When you have a definite plan to bring order out of chaos, you can begin with some confidence that you will be able to make progress. Your depression will make it difficult to move forward rapidly, but don't give up. Take small steps and understand that any progress in the right direction is a victory. The movement of your body will be beneficial to your recovery.

Seek sympathetic hands-on help with your organizing project. Various kinds of help might be available and appropriate. You may hire someone who cleans for a living and ask them to help you get things under control. Some professional organizers specialize in your kind of problem. An understanding friend or family member might be helpful.

Obtain support. There are many online support groups that will encourage you as you set small goals. They will cheer you when you move forward and bolster you when you falter. As useful as they are, online groups will not substitute for the comfort you will get from interaction with a real live person and a face-to-face meeting.

Be very nice to yourself. Have your nails done regularly. Soak in a bubble bath. Light a candle. Buy a plant or flowers. Decide what you would like to do if time, money, obligations, fatigue, and depression didn't stand in your way. Start thinking about how you can do it.

None of these things by themselves will be a giant leap forward, but they are baby steps in the right direction.

Find a reason to live. In his book *Do One Thing Different* (New York: Quill, 1999), Bill O'Hanlon tells the story of a wealthy, elderly lady who had withdrawn from life, including her church life, partly because she found it too difficult to circulate in the wheelchair she was now using. She had become depressed and was hinting at suicide. Her only interest was her hobby of growing African violets in her large greenhouse.

She was visited by psychiatrist Milton Erickson at the request of a worried nephew. Erickson looked around her place. She admitted that her depression was becoming quite serious.

Erickson told her that it was clear to him that her problem was not depression. It was that she was not being a very good Christian. She was taken aback and bristled until he explained. "Here you are with all this money, time, and ability to grow African violets, and it is all going to waste." He encouraged her to look in the church bulletin for births, marriages, funerals, and illnesses and to take a potted African violet to the people involved, offering condolences, congratulations, or encouragement as the occasion required. She agreed that she had been falling down on her Christian duty and decided to have her handyman drive her around to make her deliveries. When she died ten years later, her funeral was attended by thousands who had come to pay their respects to the charitable and caring lady known as the African violet queen of Milwaukee.

Open up to a social life. Depressed people sometimes seek to substitute computer friends for local ones. It is so much easier to sit in front of a computer in your nightgown than to call someone, get dressed, go out, and be responsible for conversation. You need to work toward keeping up personal contacts, to get a real live hug from a caring friend. You and I know that shame about our living condition acts as a convenient excuse for not forming social ties. The depression makes us reluctant to do that anyway. The house and our social lives are a package deal. As the house improves, we are able to open up to the possibilities of developing relationships, which are so much a part of any healthy lifestyle.

Assess the Mess

1. Do you think depression may be a part of your problem with the house?

2. If so, what do you feel you can do to begin to address the problem?
   a. Read more about depression?
   b. Consult a medical or mental health professional? Who might that be?
   c. Begin lifestyle changes or pursue any other of the steps suggested? Name the ones you think you will use.

10

cleanliness and godliness

Is messiness a matter of morality? Do good and righteous women keep neat houses while lazy and slovenly women live in clutter? Does God exhort those who falter in this area of life to do better?

The Bible is full of vigorous women doing many interesting things. We wonder how they could live the active lives they did and keep up their houses.

Anna, an eighty-four-year-old widow, lived at the temple, where she praised God and waited for the Messiah. Did she leave her little room as neat as a pin each morning when she went to pray? Or was her mind on heavenly matters and her room in a shambles?

What about the working woman? Deborah was a judge who held court regularly long before she went with Barak to war. What kind of house did she keep? Did her husband, Lappidoth, complain that she was spending too much time away and letting things slip at home? Or did he marvel that she was able to keep up so well with all she had to do? Did she have servants? Or did he help?

Lydia, the first European convert, was a businesswoman who sold expensive fabric. Shiphrah and Puah were full-time midwives. It seems they trained other midwives and directed them as well. Now that is a hectic schedule! Were they able to keep their homes in order?

There is also the remarkable woman of Proverbs 31. She was busy sewing, cooking, buying land, selling it for a profit, and reinvesting in farmland. In addition, she was in the wholesale garment business, making linen clothing and accessories for retail merchants. This woman was an organizer of herself and others as well.

The Bible shows us women involved in the community. On the whole, however, it shows women involved in activities related directly and specifically to women:

Giving birth, as seen in the lives of Jesus' and Moses' mothers, who both gave birth under very stressful circumstances.

Feeding their families, as seen in the poor widow who tried to feed her sons with only a little oil and meal.

Entertaining, as seen in Sarah when she entertained the angels and in Mary and Martha when they entertained Jesus and his followers.

Caring for sick children, as seen in the Shunnamite woman when her child was taken ill in the field.

Fighting illnesses of their own, as seen in the woman with the issue of blood.

Fighting grief and loss, as seen in the widow whose son died and in Mary and Martha when their brother died.

Using sex to get their way, as did Delilah with Samson.

The Bible is like a Shakespearean play, full of energetic people deeply involved in the stuff of life. Heavenly principles apply very directly to the real events of life. But not a word is spoken about housekeeping.

The Bible covers a long period and encompasses many lifestyles. Abraham and his family were nomads living in tents. Excavations from the area of Ur, where he lived before he began his nomadic life, indicate that the civilization was a gracious one. The clothing was beautiful and the jewelry elegant. The women wore elaborate makeup. Some green eye shadow was found still intact in one of the queen's golden pots.

They lived in a labor-rich society. They had lots of help. The woman of Proverbs 31 speaks of the maidens she had to help her. They did not have many goods to take care of, however. It was not easy to produce items for the house or personal use. Because they traveled frequently and lived in tents, they didn't keep junk. Besides, they did not have malls, mail-order catalogs, and credit cards, all of which make accumulation easy. Like a river, things flow into our houses, and like a dam, we try to conserve as much of it as we can. In those days one piece of clothing was considered a treasure. The use of clothing in bartering is mentioned often. One of the Israelites stole some clothing from Jericho and buried it under his tent. Samson bet several suits of clothing in an unfortunate wager with his wife's friends. The Roman soldiers gambled to see who would win Jesus' cloak, which was special because it had no seam. They were labor rich and product poor.

Our society is the opposite. We do not have much help for the work we have to do, but we have many things to care for. We are product rich and labor poor.

As the Jews later settled into their land, and life became more stable, they began to acquire more goods to take care of. Toward the end of the Old Testament, some even had both winter and summer houses. Even so, compared with our affluence, they led simple lives.

From the Bible we get clues about the way people lived in the days of Jesus. For example, Jesus told the story of the

Like a river, things flow into our houses, and like a dam, we try to conserve as much of it as we can.

woman who lost a coin and swept the room until she found it. This is one of the few stories in the Bible that even remotely refers to housework.

Mary and Martha provide us some insight into entertainment when Martha complains to Jesus that Mary is not helping her prepare the meal.

Aside from a few incidental bits of cultural information (e.g., they used their roofs for gathering places in much the same way we use porches, and they slept in bed with their families around them), the Bible gives us little insight into what God might have to say about the use or condition of our homes.

I consider this to be a good thing for Messies, who have trouble following anybody's instructions about housekeeping. At least we can be messy without violating any of our scriptural commands. This frees us to tackle the problem directly without any unnecessary recriminations that will only make it harder for us to change.

Sometimes women who wish to change look for an outside force to whip them into action. They try to use God. But God is not a whip we can use to force ourselves to clean the house. Cleanliness, though desirable, is not next to godliness.

One woman, when she wants her children to clean their rooms, asks them if they would like to have Jesus as a guest in the room when it is messy. She told me they get busy and clean it up when she says this.

Somehow this smacks of using God to obtain our own ends, which is backward. God uses us to obtain his ends. I realize that this method gets the kids busy in their rooms, but is she teaching them something about God that God does not teach about himself? Out of respect for him we should be careful not to use him for our own purposes, no matter how good our purposes are.

Well-meaning friends sometimes use what they believe is a valid spiritual approach to the problem of poor housekeeping. One Messie who has a harried schedule, four young children, and a Messie husband, mentioned to her Cleanie friend at church how much she wished for more time to work in her house.

"Well, maybe if you put the Lord first everything would fall into place," the Cleanie friend hesitantly suggested.

"The Lord blesses my house, but he doesn't do the dishes," the Messie responded. "Pardon me if that sounds irreverent, but I know lots of ungodly people with beautiful homes. I have to spend time with the Lord just to survive."

In contrast to this attitude, some Christian women take a particularly nondirective approach to their lives, believing that is the most spiritual. They awaken each day with an attitude of openness to what the day may bring from the Lord. They do not plan their own schedules or make any decision about how to handle their problems. Instead, they rely on God to solve them. Sometimes they say they are praying and waiting on God's direction.

When God created Adam and Eve, he told them to take control of the world around them. He specifically said, "Have dominion over the fish of the sea, over the birds of the air . . . and over every creeping thing that creeps on the earth" (Gen. 1:26 NKJV). A synonym for *dominion* is *control*. Men and women were created to take control of the world around them. Some people, however, especially Messies, have such a hard time making decisions that they choose this "spiritual" approach of waiting for God to decide for them. This seems to relieve them of responsibility and adds an aura of holiness. If you are waiting for God's direction, he may be directing you to take control of your life. This does not mean that you take your life out of God's control; it means that you take responsibility for yourself.

When the Bible does not speak directly to a subject, we can draw some inferences from God's whispers in creation. God looked at the work he had done and said it was good. Because we are made in God's image, we desperately want to look at our own creation and say that it is good. Disappointment in that area upsets and saddens us. We can't let messiness take over and be happy about it. It is against our natures.

God also whispered to us about the importance of relationships when he said, "It is not good for man to be alone." Messiness is not conducive to building or maintaining important family relationships.

Messiness interferes with our relationship with ourselves. When the house is messy and our lives are disorganized, we lose touch with what is peaceful and noble in ourselves, and our self-image suffers.

> Because we are made in God's image, we desperately want to look at our own creation and say that it is good.

Messiness interferes with our relationships with others. We cannot invite people to our houses and share the good things of God with them. Our children are embarrassed to invite their friends in. We don't even want the repairman to come into certain parts of our house.

Messiness interferes with our relationships with those we love. Instinctively we know that beauty and order are essential to romance. Romance cannot root in clutter. Young men and women go out of their way to look good to each other and to show a tidy, attractive home to those they are interested in.

As a teenager, Mary Lou would rather have died than have Johnny drop in when the house was a mess. Without anyone telling her, she knew that clutter puts a damper on romance. Once married, however, in the heat of living, Mary Lou forgot that. Imperceptibly, romance suffered. Johnny loves her. Their mutual interests provide them with pleasure; their mutual commitment maintains stability in their home. Romance may even grow. But it will never bloom as beautifully as it would in a relaxing and organized environment. It is a tribute to them that they do as well as they do in this hostile environment.

Messiness interferes with our relationship with God. Worship is the expression of a loving relationship with God, and it works in a way similar to romance. Adoration and praise flow much more freely and vigorously in a sunny room with shiny tables and an uncluttered rug. But Mary Lou tries to praise and adore God in a room with unfolded clothes, shoes lying about, and piles of paper on the table awaiting attention. She says to herself that she does not have any more time for God. It is not just a matter of time. The whole house is discouraging. Mary Lou turns away from God and turns on the television, where everybody has a great-looking house.

It is true that the Bible does not directly say, "Thou shalt not keep a messy house." But it is easy to see that housekeeping has an important place in our personal, family, and spiritual relationships. To develop those relationships to their fullest, we need to respect the need for beauty and order in the house. Messiness is not a moral issue. It is, however, an important personal issue. As in all important issues, God cares and is interested in helping us in our time of need.

Assess the Mess

1. If you have trouble keeping your house orderly, do you sometimes think your messiness adversely affects your relationship with God? Do you think these feelings are valid? Explain.

2. A woman in Chicago never got her work done on time because she believed it was her spiritual duty to do everything perfectly because the Bible says, "Be ye perfect." How does the spiritual dimension in your life relate to any obsessive thinking you may have?

3. Do you use your relationship with God to modify or intensify compulsive tendencies? Explain.

4. Can you think of anything not mentioned in this chapter that the Bible says about housekeeping?

5. How does the condition of your house interfere with your relationships with others, such as family, friends, and neighbors?

6. Describe the kind of place you would like to have in your home to meet with God in a worship experience.

11

to change or not to change

"I have never done that thing that I wanted to in all my life," said the character Babbitt in the last line of Sinclair Lewis's novel by the same name.

Messies have a tendency to live like Babbitt. They deny themselves as a matter of principle. Many Messies have denied their feelings so long that they are out of touch with themselves and their desires; they don't know their own tastes or what styles or colors they like. They think they need an interior decorator, but what would they tell her? It is hard for Messies to know what to buy to improve the house. They are so used to ignoring themselves that they are unaware of what they are getting along without.

This willingness to live with unmet needs may stem from a background in which a child's needs were chronically ignored. Concerning children from dysfunctional backgrounds, Gravitz and Bowden write, "These are children who will go along with any and every suggestion because they seem unwilling or incapable of making decisions. They will shrug their shoulders and say, 'It doesn't matter,' since they have no sense of their own needs. Somewhere along the line they lose that sense of power and self through a belief that they cannot affect their environment or their own lives . . . Adult children may find that acknowledging their personal needs leads them to feel guilty, because they have learned to regard their needs as an imposition on others."

One woman I met at a seminar had books lining the floor of her home and did not realize she needed a bookcase. When I suggested she get one, she looked surprised. This lack of awareness of our own needs is one reason organizational methods work only partially. They tell you what you ought to do but they don't tune you in to what you want and need to do. If you are struggling with chronic messiness, you may very well be denying yourself without even realizing it.

Learning to keep house is like learning to dance. If there is no feeling for the music, there is only mechanical movement. That's the way it is with housekeeping. Your desires are the music, and your housekeeping moves in harmony with it. Then and only then will housekeeping become more than a mechanical chore.

In medieval times dancing was a symbol for living. God was called the Lord of the Dance: "I'll lead you on wherever you may be; I'll lead you on in the dance, said he."

As we think of our lives as a dance orchestrated by the Lord of the Dance, the condition of the house takes on new meaning. Not only is it the backdrop for our lives, it becomes part of that wonderful rhythm we are privileged to participate in.

But many Messies distrust their own feelings, disrupting the joy of the movement. They fear that if they begin to think in terms of their own tastes, desires, and needs, they will become selfish and deny their higher spiritual commitments. It doesn't work that way. Denying one's feelings and tastes is what causes an unbalanced life. When we use the denial approach, we become hooked on getting more stuff, finding security in our possessions, and filling our lives so full they can never be fulfilled. Being out of touch with our feelings and needs is the reason we have all this trouble with our houses. Once we accept our wants and needs, the house comes into balance.

We are nearing the moment of decision when you will have to choose between changing and not changing, between order and disorder, between beauty and chaos, between balance and unbalance. To prepare for that decision, you must get in touch with your own desires. Which of these lifestyles do you want? Consider the following reasons for getting your house under control and check the ones that express your desires.

> Learning to keep house is like learning to dance. If there is no feeling for the music, there is only mechanical movement.

Reasons to Get the House under Control

1. **So the house will look better for company.** It is embarrassing to have people come over with the house in a mess. When you work like crazy to hide the disorder, you have to keep some messy parts off limits. You fear they will go into a messy part. That fearfulness takes the joy out of having visitors. You also want to be able to call a repairman and not be embarrassed to let him in. He's not company, but still . . .

2. **So the house will look nice for you.** You are tired of living in all this clutter and ugliness. It wears you out to see it all the time. Although you have gotten used to it to some extent and you try to accept it, living like this takes a lot out of life.

3. **So the house will work better.** When you can't find things, when you have to move one thing to put another down, when you don't have enough supplies for what you want to do, the house is not working right. You want a cooperative house.

4. **For a special friend.** You want to have your boyfriend over, but you don't want him to see how you live. You want

to believe that if he really cares for you, he won't care how the house looks, but you know that's not true. How the house looks reflects on you personally, even if you don't think it should.

5. **So you can decorate.** You know it is ridiculous to bring lovely things into your house the way it is. Sometimes you try, but your special things never look pretty because of the clutter.

6. **So you can get out without feeling guilty.** For a long time you have had ambivalent feelings about leaving the house. On the one hand, you have denied yourself many outings to stay home and "do something about this house." On the other hand, you have looked for opportunities to do things outside the house just to get away from it. You want to get the house in order so you can stay in it happily or, if you wish, leave without feeling guilty.

> Messies live from one crisis to another. . . . Crisis-oriented living keeps you in a constant state of activity, which makes you feel alive and useful.

7. **So you won't have to work so hard.** People who don't have messy houses don't seem to work as hard as you do. Doing the simplest job is a big deal in your house. You spend a lot of time looking for things. Just getting dressed can be a chore because you have to locate the clothes in all the disorganization. You want life to be easier.

8. **To get others off your back.** Others are constantly nagging about how the house looks. Perhaps your husband has threatened to leave unless you get it cleaned up. Perhaps he has already left.

9. **Legal reasons.** Some Messies run into legal trouble because of their messiness. Husbands have used their wife's disorganized lifestyle as a way to gain custody of the children. And sometimes neighbors call, or threaten to call, the zoning, fire, or health departments because they are concerned about the health risk or because they are repulsed by how bad the yard looks.

10. **To overcome depression.** Life is hardly worth living when you feel as bad as this cluttered house makes you feel.

Your self-esteem has hit bottom. You want emotional release from the depression, guilt, and anger you feel.

Reasons to Leave the House Messy

1. **Lost hope.** The job of changing looks too big. You don't see any hope of success. It is better not to try than to put all that energy and hope into it and fail.

2. **It takes too much work.** You are the laid-back type. You don't have the attention span or a high enough level of interest to keep the house nice.

3. **Trouble with the family.** You want to change, but does your family? They would have a fit if they had to put their things away and keep the house nice.

4. **Destroy your creativity.** You do not want to lose the creativity that is linked to your messiness. You believe messy people are more creative. And more interesting too!

5. **Priority of other interests.** Keeping the house in order is not one of your priorities. You have other interests, other things you would rather spend your time and energy on.

6. **Change of self-image.** You think of yourself as messy and disorganized. Who would you be if you changed? Would you suffer some kind of identity crisis?

7. **You don't believe in self-indulgence.** If you start thinking in terms of your own needs and of improving the house so it will be nicer, you might get carried away and become self-centered. You believe it is safer from a spiritual standpoint not to concentrate too much on how the house looks. Other things are more deserving of your time, effort, and interests.

8. **Costs too much.** Getting the house in order would cost too much money, and you have other uses for it. Education, travel, and cultural pursuits matter more. They last forever. Furniture and labor-saving devices are only temporary.

9. **Loss of excuses.** The house has been your excuse for not doing other things. Once you get the house in order, there

will be no end to what you feel obligated to do. You might also feel obligated to invite more people to your house, and you're not sure you want to do that.

10. **You don't deserve a nice house.** Some people are worthy of a nice house, but you think you don't deserve one. So why work at it?

11. **To feel needed.** If the house gets organized you will have nothing else to do, so you will not feel needed.

12. **To exert your authority.** You have a perfect way to exert your will over someone else. They want you to clean the house. You don't. So when the house is messy, you win.

13. **To punish someone.** You use the messy house to get back at somebody. You know you can upset them by keeping a messy house, so you do.

14. **To test your friendships.** Those who like you in spite of your house are true friends. You can test your friends' sincerity by bringing them into the house. If they like the real you, the house doesn't matter.

15. **Inability to organize.** Some people have a knack for organizing, but you don't know where to begin or how to continue.

16. **Fear of making a mistake.** Suppose you throw away something important. Suppose you set up an organizational system that doesn't work. It is better not to make a change than to make mistakes. You don't want to live with regrets.

17. **Crisis-oriented living.** It is the nature of a Messie to live from one crisis to another. You organize your life to ensure that you will always have a crisis of some kind. If none occurs naturally, you will create one. Crisis-oriented living keeps you in a state of constant activity, which makes you feel alive and useful. It's that old adrenaline rush again. And all of this activity and chaos keeps you too busy to deal with the more resistant areas of life you wish to avoid anyway.

18. **Diversionary tactic.** Struggling with clutter is a way to avoid our emotions. As long as it is an issue in our lives, we

don't have to deal with more important things like relationships, family, and health.

19. **Staves off boredom.** As long as there is clutter, there is something to fill time or at least occupy one's mind. It avoids the tedium of having nothing to do. One Messie who was considering giving up the cluttered lifestyle asked, "If I get the house in order, what will I do with my time?" That is an insightful question.

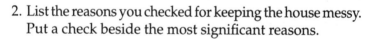

Assess the Mess

1. List the reasons you checked for getting your house in order. Add any others you think of. Put a check beside the strongest reasons.

   a.

   b.

   c.

   d.

   e.

2. List the reasons you checked for keeping the house messy. Put a check beside the most significant reasons.

   a.

   b.

   c.

   d.

   e.

3. When you look at the second list, you will see that most of your reasons for keeping your house messy involve fears. Earlier in the book I mentioned that Messies have more emotional involvement with their houses than successful housekeepers have. Messies love their things more intensely. They fear more often and more strongly. It is fear most of all that paralyzes the Messie who de-

voutly wishes she could change. What fears keep you from getting the house in order?

a.
b.
c.

4. Think of ways to overcome these fears and free yourself to get and keep your house in order. List three steps you might take to overcome the fears that are holding you back.

a.
b.
c.

5. When did you first notice a problem keeping the house in order?

6. How did you first notice it?

7. What happened when you first tried to change?

8. What kept you from success?

9. What has hindered you since that time?

10. Are the reasons the same as the original ones or different?

The Choice Is Yours

Leaving the house messy is a viable choice, but it is hard for me to offer it when I know the pain it will bring. While writing this chapter, I spoke to a Messie from Pennsylvania. She has four children; the youngest is seven weeks old. She said she was going to kill herself if she did not get help. Although she said it with a laugh, she wasn't entirely joking. The comment expressed her frustration and impatience with the problem.

She is a member of another anonymous group but has not been able to get control of her house by using the group's twelve-step method. She thought she could be successful if she just worked harder and longer, even though her neighbors seemed to be sitting around in their lovely homes not working. To speed herself up to get more done she took diet pills. This was not good for her, nor did she feel that it was wise for a mother with young children to take them. She was willing to do almost anything to change. She knew the Serenity Prayer: "God, grant me the serenity to accept the things I cannot change, Courage to change the things I can, and Wisdom to know the difference." Her problem, she said, was that she was unable to change and unwilling to accept herself. "I just can't accept this in myself," she said. The truth was that she was able to accept herself as a Messie (she had been doing it daily, albeit unhappily), and she was also able to change. But she did not know that yet.

You may choose to have a messy house. If you do, you know what ills to expect. If you choose to have an orderly and beautiful house, you do not yet know what problems or joys await you. I assure you, however, that you will feel as if a weight has been lifted when your life turns around, not because your house is nice, though that is a wonderful thing, but because you have a sense of control.

Your choice will also bring new problems. You will make mistakes, but as Walt Whitman said, "The man who can't make a mistake, can't make anything."

According to a fable, a roguish young man heard of a sage who was said to know the hearts of men and discern things not known to others. To draw attention to his own wisdom, the young man decided to discredit the sage by testing him in such a way that he would have to be wrong. He told his young companions about his plan. He would get a live bird and hold it behind him. He would then ask the sage whether the bird was dead or alive. If the sage said the bird was dead, the young man would show him the bird alive. If the sage said the bird was alive, he would squeeze it to death behind him and show the sage the dead bird.

On the appointed day the young man met the sage with his companions looking on. "Oh, great sage," he began, "in my hand I hold a bird. Tell me, is the bird dead or is it alive?"

The sage, who was indeed wise, looked at the young man and at his companions, all waiting for an answer. The young man's scheme was obvious to the sage, so he answered, "The bird is as you will, young man. It is as you will."

It is as you will.

You hold the fate of the house in your hands, and the house will be as you will.

Look at the two lists—the reasons to change and the reasons not to change. Which is more powerful in your life? Saying "yes" to neatness is like saying "I do" in marriage. We know something of the commitment we are making, but there are many details we are not aware of. You know what the messy life is like. You do not know what the orderly life is like. You see what it is like for your friends, but you do not know what it will be like for you. As Shakespeare said in Hamlet, we often would "rather bear those ills we have than fly to others that we know not of."

If you have not marked another part of this book, mark this spot. You have four choices:

1. Remain messy and quit fighting it.
2. Remain messy and hate every minute of it.
3. Keep trying harder and working smarter by using organizational methods to make the house neat.
4. Have an orderly house without struggling with new organizational methods.

The last choice sounds too good to be true, but it is the only one that works. And it works almost like a magic wand because it acts in conjunction with what we really want to do. When we get in touch with that secret, we have a kind of magic. Part 2 of this book tells you how to take hold of your magic wand.

part 2

overcoming the messie mind-set

Part 2 covers how to overcome the Messie mind-set. It explores such subjects as why organizational systems don't work, why working harder doesn't work, how to handle the messy family, and how to overcome the stress of living in a disorganized way.

12

living the orderly life

A young man from a small Midwestern town graduated at the top of his high school class and applied to the state university, even though the idea of going to a large school terrified him. Sure, he was a big fish in his small pond, but was he really college material? He filled out the college entrance forms, took the entrance exam, and waited for his scores. The results confirmed his worst fears. Although he had been accepted, he was only average in intelligence, perhaps slightly below.

He made miserable grades in his college classes and was about to leave school when his advisor called him in. Why, he wanted to know, was an A student suddenly making Ds? The young man explained that his low IQ of 98 made it impossible for him to succeed in the classes he was taking. Flabbergasted, the advisor explained the 98 was not his IQ but the percentile in which he ranked among all the students who had taken the entrance exam. This information freed the young man. From then on he was back to his straight-A performance.

As we see from this example, having the ability is not enough. We must also know we have the ability before we will be able to use it. One of the problems of looking closely at our abilities, or lack of them, is that we may get the impression that we are unable to get the house in order.

The Orderly Person Within

Even calling ourselves "Messies" may give us the wrong impression of ourselves and make us think we are unable to get the house in order. Nothing could be further from the truth. Getting a house under control requires nothing that we do not have or cannot get. You have an orderly person within you. That is why you are reading this book. You want to let that orderly person out. You need to shift your attention from the messy person's thinking, which has dominated your life, to the orderly person's thinking.

It takes time to make that change. Old thoughts and habits do not melt away overnight. When you approach a closet, drawer, or pile of clothes, do it with detachment. Be good to yourself. Refuse to saddle yourself with all kinds of unnecessary junk because of fear. You know that life is full of things for you; therefore you do not need to grasp every scrap to satisfy yourself.

A New Way of Thinking

There are two kinds of thin people: those who are thin and never think about it and those who are thin and are always fighting to stay that way. Many Messies have attained a degree of success in housekeeping, but it is a daily struggle to maintain it because it goes against the grain of what they really want to do. When the Messie ceases struggling and instead begins thinking of order as her primary desire, success begins. The rest of this book is about getting into that mode of thinking and leaving the old, fearful, unsuccessful one behind.

My own experience with being a Messie has been lengthy. When I first realized what I had been doing to myself, I became angry. This anger propelled me into a search for help. The help I found became the basis for my Messies Anonymous program. When I began the program, things started to improve immediately. Order and beauty emerged. Within two weeks, I could see a difference. But basically I was still thinking in the old way while trying to act in a new way. My old way of thinking put obstacles in the way of freedom. However, when I discovered the successful average housekeeper mentality (discussed in chapter 14) things began to change more effortlessly. Old bastions of resistance began to crack, and order poured out. The solutions to problems that had remained obscure became clear.

> Having the ability is not enough. We must also know we have the ability before we will be able to use it.

Many Messies who have used the Messies Anonymous program successfully will be further helped by this book. Those who haven't used the M.A. approach will find release from the Messie lifestyle not found by those who change their housekeeping habits without fully changing their thinking.

Be patient with yourself. You are not doing this for your spouse, family, friends, parents, or anybody but yourself. You do not have to prove anything to yourself and certainly not to them. Be prepared to slip. When the change begins, the Messie part of you will see itself shrinking and will try to get you to turn back. It will try to sabotage your success and go back to the more comfortable and familiar Messie lifestyle. But don't give in.

Many times I was tempted to go back to the old way. The only thing that kept me going was my unwillingness to return to the pain of living that way. My family, whom I had trained to be messy, put up many obstacles. But I, like many others, have found freedom to live in order and beauty.

You do not need discipline or commitment to succeed with this program. All you need is a vision of yourself as a person of worth and dignity living in a way that reflects those qualities. Once this vision is in place, a peculiar thing begins to happen. When all the forces of sky and earth that have been at work against you see that you will not abandon your dream, they will finally give up and say to each other, "It's not worth it! Let her have her dream!" and they will slink away.

When you let the successful housekeeper out, she will do the job for you. The chapters that follow tell you how to give her freedom.

more discipline doesn't work

"How many psychiatrists does it take to change a light bulb?"

"One, but the light bulb has to want to be changed."

This is true of any change we wish to make in our lives. Change comes only when we really want to be changed.

Many Messies are motivated by the idea of a new way of life and will make many changes. They will buy new curtains, get new bookshelves, and give away clutter, but they hold back in challenging a few ways of thinking. The most important change we need to make is in our thinking. Until we do, we will contend with the stress of living in two worlds.

Just as overweight people seek thinness and alcoholics seek sobriety, Messies search for order. Just as smokers look for relief from their habit and gamblers wish to be free of their uncontrollable drive, Messies want to be free of the clutter and disorder that characterize their lives.

The Place of Emotions

Messies are very emotional people. Emotions get them going one day and bring them to a halt the next. Any approach that is going to work for chronically disorganized people is going to have to take emotions into account.

You can change, but you must want it.

This high emotional involvement is why Messies do not respond well to pragmatic approaches to orderliness. If they try to use a pragmatic, systematic approach that involves pure willpower to overcome their weaknesses, they may meet with initial success but will probably fall back into the same old patterns of messiness and disorganization. The only thing that will be different after such a failure will be feelings of increased hopelessness.

Messies are wonderful people. They are enthusiastic, deep, conscientious, full of fun, interesting, interested in many things, and successful in many areas of their lives—but they are failures when it comes to organization.

How Discipline Works

Because of these common characteristics of Messies, the words willpower and self-discipline are never heard in the Messies Anonymous vocabulary or used in the M.A. program. Messies do not respond well to approaches based on these concepts. I believe, in fact, that most people do not respond well to these concepts. People talk about discipline as though it is a powerful force in changing behavior. This is mainly talk. Discipline is highly overrated as a factor in achievement.

We do see discipline at work in the military. Young people who may never have been disciplined in their lives quickly become disciplined under the influence of the boot camp drill sergeant. Things they may never have done and never expected to have to do, they do regularly in the military. They may not want to make their beds or shine their shoes, but they do. That is discipline: doing what you don't want to do. The reason they do it, of course, is because they don't want to get in trouble. They may be totally undisciplined off the base. When they go home, they may not make their beds or shine their shoes. But for a short time, with the sergeant's supervision, they are disciplined.

> Discipline is highly overrated as a factor in achievement.

We also see discipline in the lives of artists, both in fine arts and the performing arts. We see it in the lives of athletes. To excel in their fields, artists and athletes put in long hours of hard work, excluding other interests and demands on their time, so they may someday paint a masterpiece, play in Carnegie Hall, or go to the Olympics. Further inspection will show us, however, that this discipline may not be a part of their lives in every aspect. Athletes who discipline themselves for their sport may live a wild and unruly life when practice is over.

When we look at people who exhibit great discipline in their lives, we see that it is generally in one area, and sometimes, as in the case of athletes, it is for a limited period of time.

But what about everyday discipline? There are people who live well-ordered lives. Their checkbooks are always up to date, their houses are tidy, their cars are washed, and their laundry is folded and put away. They seem to do this effortlessly while others (the undisciplined ones, we assume) are running amuck trying to keep their houses within the allowable range of clutter. Why is this?

Need More Willpower?

Many people think discipline is the result of willpower. They say things like "I can't lose weight because I don't have enough willpower," "I need more willpower to stop smoking,"

"I could stop gambling if I had enough willpower," or, as many of us say, "I just don't have enough willpower to keep up with the house. I need to be more disciplined."

Rather than willpower and discipline, Messies need focus.

It does not help to quote platitudes such as "Where there is a will there is a way" to the floundering Messie. It does not help to tell her to have a stronger will, to put her nose to the grindstone and her shoulder to the wheel. Platitudes just cause confusion and guilt. They may be true, but they are not the answer to the Messie's problem. Telling a Messie these things is like telling a man whose car is immobilized by transmission problems that using high-octane gasoline will make it run better. It may be true that higher octane gas makes cars run more smoothly, but that does not help him because his problem has nothing to do with combustion.

Admonishing someone to be more disciplined or have stronger willpower helps only those whose lives are already running pretty well. It does not get to the root of the Messie's problem. She must get something else fixed before she can even begin to consider the place discipline may have in her life.

Focus Is the Secret

Rather than willpower and discipline, Messies need focus. Messies are not generally focused on what they want to do in the house. They only want things better in some foggy sense. If you are able to focus on what it is you want to do for your house, the house will begin to change automatically. The discipline and willpower will come if they are needed.

Focus is an interesting thing. With simple adjustments photographers can change the focus of a picture from the foreground to the background. With the foreground in focus, the background disappears in a blur. Likewise, successful housekeepers who focus clearly on their homes have learned to leave secondary things out of focus.

The problem with Messies is that many things keep their interest in lovely homes out of focus. Practicality, for example, distorts focus. Many practical ideas mess up the house. You may want a stationary bicycle for exercise. Where better to put it than in the living room? Your mother-in-law is giving away some furniture. You take it, even though you don't need it, because you hope someday to move into a larger place where you can use it. In the meantime your family is using small paths to get through the crowded house. You can vegetables but have no place to store the jars, so you stack them on your kitchen counter for the winter. Or perhaps you stack the empty canning jars on the kitchen counter in case you decide to can in the future. All these practical ideas end up making the house untidy and hard to live in.

The next distracter Messies need to watch out for is any activity that conflicts with the care of a beautiful home. Sometimes these activities seem as though they will add beauty to the home, but they clutter it instead. Crafts, for instance, can undermine beauty. A Messie who wants to beautify her home may take a tole painting or cross-stitching class. Many of her friends do it. She can socialize and make something nice for her house. The project may turn out lovely, but few people will appreciate its beauty if the house is a mess because she has left her supplies out.

The time and money spent on tole painting or cross-stitching would have been better spent on bringing the main part of the house into focus. She has been working hard to improve the house, and she wonders why it doesn't look any better than before. She does not realize that her time was misspent because it was unfocused.

Sometimes this lack of focus is at the heart of the interior decorating problem. The Messie gathers such a variety of eclectic materials that no style or color scheme dominates. People say to her, "Your house is so interesting." But no one says her house is lovely. She has all the necessary pieces; they just don't work together. She needs to realize that some wonderful but unmatched things must go if a beautiful and orderly house is to emerge. You do not need discipline or willpower to make your life organized and successful. You only need to know how to focus your attention and effort where it will make a difference.

Maintaining Focus

What appears to be willpower is actually want power. People who keep nice houses focus on their desire for a lovely and orderly home. They don't have to strive to get their houses to conform. The houses just do. They do not have a white-hot, burning passion for a perfect house. They just have a comfortable, warm desire for a nice one. It never occurs to them to settle for less. Why should it? For them it is no struggle to maintain their homes as they want them, because they maintain their focus.

As mentioned before, when we bring one part of the picture into focus, it makes other parts fuzzy. When we begin to emphasize the house, other areas of life will get less attention. To focus our attention in productive ways, we must decide which unnecessary things we are doing that focus our attention away from the overall order and beauty of our houses. When we eliminate these, our lives will be disciplined without having to use willpower and without having to keep our noses to the grindstone.

Sometimes we need others to help us focus on what we want and to keep our commitment in focus. Friends, or a group of friends (perhaps an M.A. self-help group), can help us verbalize our desires and thereby sharpen our focus. We will have a force even stronger than willpower—a sharply focused want power.

Assess the Mess

1. Do you suffer from lack of focus as it relates to your house? Explain.

2. One Messie told me that one day when she could no longer stand her messy house, she cleaned the ceiling fan first, even though the house was so cluttered she could hardly find a place on the floor for the chair she needed to stand on to do the job. The needs of the house were out of focus. Describe several incidents that illustrate your lack of focus.

   a.
   b.
   c.

3. Name several things that diffuse your attention (e.g., hobbies, children's activities, volunteer activities, practicality). Explain briefly. Put a check beside the ones you can give up or do more moderately.

   a.
   b.
   c.

4. Using want power, describe what you actually want for your house if money, time, energy, and other problems were not a consideration.

14

working harder doesn't work

Horatio Alger Jr., a nineteenth-century American minister and novelist, wrote about 120 books for boys. Most of Alger's characters were poor bootblacks or newsboys whose virtue and hard work were invariably rewarded with riches and success. Some people believe that Alger's books contributed to the American belief that hard work always results in success. Perhaps they also contributed to a similar but more dangerous mind-set—that laziness is always the cause of failure.

J. Paul Getty, U.S. oil executive and millionaire, knew that success involves a lot more than just hard work. In response to a request from a magazine for a short article explaining his success, Getty wrote: "Some people find oil. Others don't."

Getty recognized that it was not working harder that had earned his wealth. In the same way that working harder doesn't always make us rich, it doesn't always make us neat either. But Messies are programmed to think that laziness is to blame for their lack of housekeeping success. They try to think of themselves as imaginative or interesting, but the word *lazy* keeps echoing in the back of their minds.

Occasionally you will see an article about the problem of collecting too much and having clutter all around. Usually these articles are written tongue-in-cheek. The author is trying to show that she is a bit eccentric. But hey! That just makes her all the more lovable, doesn't it? Andy Rooney is one of those people—messy but affable.

> Messies already work hard enough. Some Messies work harder than successful housekeepers.

Long ago people laughed at drunks. They would imitate their stumbling and show how funny it was that they couldn't get the key in the lock or speak without a slur. Those jokes are no longer fashionable because people see drunkenness for the serious problem it is. Fat people used to be thought of as jolly. Now we know that many overweight people laugh only to cover their tears. Messiness is still a joke to many people. But it is not funny to the people who have it.

Messies want a life of order and dignity. They don't want to look forever for the flashlight, hammer, or keys. They don't want to live in a messy environment. They want to lead comfortable, controlled lives. And so they search for methods to overcome their madness. Some methods don't work at all; others work for a while and then falter. These methods all fall under the category of the Work Harder Approach.

The Work Harder Approach acknowledges all kinds of reasons for disorder: the size of the house, the number of people in it, the number of activities, the lack of cooperation from others. But in the end, the responsibility falls on one person—you. And if the house is not in order, you believe it is because you have not worked hard enough.

Those who try the Work Harder Approach use willpower, rules, and systematic methods. They believe that if they discover the right method and use it faithfully, their problem will be over. They think something is wrong with them because their house is not under control, and they believe it even more strongly when messiness overcomes them again. They blame themselves, not the method, for their failure.

Some of the premises of the Work Harder Approach are:

1. **Clutter is bad.** They are convinced that cleanliness is next to godliness or some modification of that slogan. Good people are neat. Bad people are slobs.

2. **Organization is an endless chore.** Some programs use lists, cards, or a variation of the two. These bring some order out of the chaos, but they also confirm to the Messie what she suspected—housecleaning is a gigantic chore. With an extra large dose of determination she tackles the system, but she eventually slips back into the clutter of the old way of life. Now she has to deal not only with the hassle of disorganized living but also with the disappointment of failure. She is now certain that she is at fault.

3. **The cleaning marathon will do the trick.** Sometimes the frustration of living in this yucky house gets to be such a hassle that the Messie goes on a cleaning binge. Everything out! Everything put away! One of the chief problems Messies have is the urge to do a lot fast. She takes two or three days to clean the house for company, and for one day the things she stuffed into drawers, closets, and cabinets stay there. On the next day they burst out, and the house returns to its normal state, or worse.

The Messie feels two things—pride that for a moment she had a lovely house and disappointment that she was not able to maintain it for more than a day.

In *Flowers for Algernon,* a mentally retarded young man is cured of his retardation. But then the treatment begins to wear off, and he returns to his retarded condition. We grieve with him as he sees himself faltering. We leave the theater sad. Messies live that story again and again as they try to function normally, only to fall back into their old ways. The cleaning marathon just leads to more failure.

4. **Self-denial is a part of good housekeeping.** Subconsciously Messies believe that to have a clean house they will have to give up the things they love to do. They are convinced there is not time enough to do the fun things or the important things and have a clean house as well. Most Messies aren't willing to sacrifice their way of life for neatness.

But self-denial, in its own way, is also a part of the Messie lifestyle, though few realize it. Messies already deny themselves every day. They deny themselves the pleasure of inviting people to their house because they are embarrassed by the mess. They also deny themselves the food they like to eat because they never have the necessary ingredients to make it. And some even deny themselves the pleasures of outside activities because they feel guilty leaving the house in such terrible condition.

5. **Working harder will bring about the change you want.** The trouble with this approach is that working harder will never bring to light the reasons you are messy. Messies already work hard enough. Some work harder than successful housekeepers. Until we uncover the underlying causes of messiness, the house will never change.

Clarence Darrow, a renowned U.S. lawyer, recognized early that hard work wasn't the only road to success. Darrow was interviewed for a magazine article about how prominent men achieved their success. "Most of the men I've spoken to so far attribute their success to hard work," said the interviewer.

"I guess that applies to me too," said Darrow. "I was brought up on a farm. One very hot day I was distributing and packing down the hay which a stacker was constantly dumping on top of me. By noon I was completely exhausted. That afternoon I left the farm, never to return, and I haven't done a day of hard work since."

Take the Easy Road

M. Scott Peck began his book *The Road Less Traveled* with the words, "Let's face it, life is difficult." That is true in some areas of life, but it does not apply to the area of overcoming disorder in your life. If it is done right, it's easy.

Those who strive only perpetuate the problem. Messies try too hard, care about too many things too much, try to dot too many i's and cross too many t's. Being perfectionists, they live lives that are unbalanced and uptight. This approach is carried over to solving the problem of clutter. That is the hard approach.

The easy approach is this: awaken to the idea that much of what Messies have been striving so hard to accomplish doesn't really matter. If the fire or flood so many Messies dream of were to destroy the belongings that drag them down, they would be much better off.

In the introduction to *Do Less, Accomplish More*, Dennis Waitley states the problem well:

> We have everything going for us but too little coming together. . . . Most of us have houses, but not the domestic lives we long for. We have photo albums and videotapes of our children, but not the spiritual strength that underpins healthy families. We are extremely busy, sometimes frantically busy, but we don't quite know where we're going. We cope with the urgent, but keep putting off what is truly important. We try to squeeze in lots of fun, sometimes expensive fun, but we're not really happy. Some of us are doing the right things at the wrong time; some are doing the wrong things all the time.

The Twelve Steps of Messies Anonymous, which have been adapted from Alcoholics Anonymous, start with the statement, "We admitted we were powerless over clutter and disorganization and that our lives had become unmanageable." A later step states, "We came to believe that a power greater than ourselves was able to restore us to sanity." These two statements say, "I give up! The way of life I have been pursuing with all these belongings and activities is absolutely crazy."

For some people, this will come as an astounding spiritual awakening. They will stop striving so hard to control their lives. They will perceive the world as full of loving abundance and will turn their lives over to the care of God. They will see their belongings as just so much junk, hire a backhoe (or the metaphorical equivalent), and walk away from this madness. For them sanity will come pretty much in one lump sum, and the house will soon reflect it.

Others will assent to the idea, but each day will be a struggle to live it out. Sanity will be eked out a little at a time, but it will come. It will come with baby steps.

Assess the Mess

Messies are perfectionists who frequently make a big deal out of everything and want to get every answer exactly right. But for these exercises, don't be particular. The first impulse will be the best. Write down what comes to your mind first.

1. When you have tried to get the house in order in the past, what has happened?

2. What approaches have you used in the past, and how well have they worked?

3. Look at the characteristics of the Work Harder Approach. Which ones involve you? Describe your experiences.

   a.
   b.
   c.

4. What is your personal response to the idea that, with a change of focus, getting and keeping your house in order can be easy?

15

arresting mess stress

A messy life is a stressful life. It is stressful for many reasons, most of which have to do with the issue of control. When you can't find your keys, or worse, your IRS papers when you are being audited, that's stress. When your children won't help around the house, or worse, keep making messes for you to clean up, that's stress. When your husband is the biggest messer in the family and tells you to relax and leave everybody alone about putting things away, that is big-time stress.

When you hate to come home (and so does everybody else) because of how it looks and how hard it is to get stuff done there, when you vow that you are going to make a change and your house *will* be organized, and it not only doesn't get better but deteriorates as you pull stuff out of their hiding places to "organize" them, you become even more aware of how cluttered and unmanageable your life is.

When you dream of your house burning down to free you from this burden, when you look wistfully at new houses and wish you could start over fresh and empty, when you would like to have a full-time houseboy to keep up your new place, you are experiencing house stress.

There is more to it than the house. You have too much to do and too little time, energy, motivation, and probably ability to do it. Because you can't keep up with what is going on, you live with the feeling that just around the curve, you will find an unpleasant surprise you should have been prepared for—but weren't. Life, not just the house, is out of control.

What Stress Looks Like

Because stress is hard to measure, making a definitive medical judgment about it is difficult. However, the American College of Physicians has put together the following checklist of symptoms that indicate a person may be under stress and should see a doctor for advice. Of course, these symptoms may be related to many other physical causes.

- Heart palpitations, chest pains, tightness in the chest
- Fear of leaving the house
- Insomnia or excessive sleeping
- Loss of interest in usual activities
- Fatigue, headaches, or other physical symptoms
- Sadness or morbid thoughts
- Worsening of existing illness without a clear explanation

Other lists include many of the degenerative diseases the body is not able to ward off because it is working so hard on the stress issue.

Other subclinical symptoms may be signs of stress:

- Increased forgetfulness (locking yourself out of the car, forgetting appointments or mixing them up, increased messiness). Stress tends to accentuate whatever weaknesses we already have. That is why Messies tend to become more disorganized, forgetful, distractible, and messy under stress. A Cleanie becomes more fanatically neat under stress.

- Anthropomorphizing inanimate objects. Belongings take on a life of their own. You feel that you must protect them and that they are out of your control. They go (get lost) and come (get found) on their own.
- Repeated colds, flu, and so on. Stress weakens our resistance to disease.
- Skin problems
- Being easily upset by unpleasant things that happen

These are symptoms that doctors and psychologists describe and analyze. We may recognize stress as the point where we feel tired of people asking too much of us, tired of asking too much of ourselves, tired of working too hard, tired of not being appreciated. In short, we are just plain tired of being so stressed out.

The Result of Stress

The symptoms of chest pain, forgetfulness, and fatigue are likely to get our attention, but stress causes many results that can go unnoticed for a long time.

What you don't see going on in your body is your tense muscles, furrowed brow, clenched jaw, and racing heart. Your body shuts down water flow, causing dryness in the mouth. Blood flow is restricted. Adrenaline pours into the system, and other glands react to it. Externally, we are going about our business. Internally, our bodies are fighting to keep things on an even keel. We become so used to it we think our bodies feel that way naturally. Nothing could be further from the truth.

The physical, emotional, and spiritual results of stress are significant. Stress requires our attention to find a solution.

Two Kinds of Stressed-Out Women

One kind of woman who is under stress is the controller. She is under stress because neither people nor things will cooperate as completely as she wants. Controllers control for a couple of reasons. First, they are afraid of things that are out of control. Second, they simply like the power of being in control.

Messies are not usually controllers of that kind, but they relate to their messiness in a controlling way and so bring pressure on themselves. No one is allowed to touch their things or to make any changes in the house that will involve their things. Woe to the reforming Messie wife who has to tackle a controlling Messie husband as well as the messy house.

The second type of woman under stress is the pleaser. Pleasers want life to go well for everybody. That is one reason they keep so many things. It is not only so that they will be well supplied; they want to have whatever anyone else will ever need as well.

Many of these people use their many skills to please others and often become very successful in their jobs. The truth is, however, that although they are capable, friendly, and highly thought of, they have very low self-esteem. That's why they try so hard to please everyone. If they are going to be successful at this impossible task, they must not make any mistakes. To make sure everyone likes them, they say "yes" to every job they are asked to do. They carry more of the load in the family than anyone. They may even go out searching for more activities to confirm that they are worthwhile people.

In short, to keep up their image of perfection and to avoid criticism (to which they are very sensitive), pleasers abandon control of their lives and priorities for the sake of others. Since pleaser women are likely to marry controller men, their lives are frequently overstocked with jobs and responsibilities given to them by their husbands. Although they may complain about being taken advantage of, they are committed to this self-destructive way of life.

Both of these approaches are unsatisfactory. To expect to be fully in control is foolish. To give up control that is appropriately ours to others is equally foolish. We can't control every aspect of our lives, but there is a point at which we must face our responsibilities and feel that we have the ability to meet them. Finding this balance is the thrust of the Serenity Prayer, in which we ask God for three things: serenity to accept what is out of our control, courage to change that which is within our control, and wisdom to figure out which is which. I think the prayer should be called the Wisdom Prayer because wisdom is probably the most difficult to attain of the three things sought.

Some Stuff Really Is out of Our Control

Studies indicate that the feeling of helplessness in controlling one's life is a major source of stress. If a dog in your neighborhood is barking loudly, you may become nervous and feel jumpy. If you are trying to sleep, each bark is like a hammer in your head. You wonder why the owners don't make the dog stop barking. If you are the owner, however, the dog's barking may not disturb you nearly as much. Why not? Because you are in control. You know that you can call the dog in and get relief from the noise. Because you know you have the power to change the annoyance, it doesn't bother you in the same way.

You may have noticed the same phenomenon in restaurants or church when young children make disturbing noises. The parents sit blithely by, seemingly oblivious to the racket. Yes, they are used to the noise of their own children and, therefore, are not as easily distracted by it. But they also know they have some control over the situation, and this relieves their stress about it.

Some aspects of your house may indeed be out of your control. Maybe it is too small for your family or too large for your strength. Maybe you don't have money to hire needed help or buy needed organizational products. Or your work schedule is very tight, and you have little time.

I don't want to negate the mountains you may be facing. However, I am always amazed to see how people are able to overcome obstacles, usually by focusing on their goals and by prayer, perseverance, alertness to options, and pure determination. Like Jacob, they will not let go until they are blessed with the desire of their hearts.

Somewhere they got the wisdom to see that they did not need courage to accept their situation. They needed courage to change it.

Help for the Stressed-Out Messie

I saw a bumper sticker that said "I Can Have It All." I should have looked to see if the driver was a frazzled wreck. If she wasn't, she was probably at the beginning stage of having it all. People at that point are still full of energy and excitement. Life is full of wonderful things to do and be and have. Messies understand the sentiment. Being wonderful people who appreciate the good, creative things in life, we don't want to miss any. We get high on having it all. When it's out there, it's hard not to go for it. We are able to do a lot more than we should. That idea is hard to accept.

At the middle stage of having it all, some stress begins to show. But the excited "haver" still believes that if she just organizes things a little tighter, she can fit them all in. Her time for herself is the first thing to go, of course. But no matter; these other things are all so much more important.

At the final stage of having it all, things begin to get out of control. One meeting cancels another. An obligation makes it impossible to go to the children's program. Nothing seems important anymore. Cooking has been greatly curtailed so she can meet her obligations. She videotaped some television programs she really wanted to see, but she has no time to watch them. They are just another pressure.

A woman in the final stage might not look frazzled because she is trying to keep up a good face. Many people would say she is successful. She hardly recognizes that she is not. She looks okay on the surface, but inside she is ragged. She will eventually feel the effects of the stress she has put herself under because she did not know the one secret of avoiding stress. Instead of trying to have it all, she should have been learning to set priorities, the secret of stress prevention.

Messies resist setting priorities. They want to avoid the decisions necessary for setting priorities, and they don't like saying "no" to a worthy cause. They recognize the needs of the world and want to help. And some of their activities bring in extra money. They wouldn't want to have to give that up. In short, Messies want to believe the "I Can Have It All" bumper sticker, but it's a lie.

Nobody can have it all. We must set priorities according to what is important and not be lured from our commitment. Picture the bumper sticker that says "I Can Have It All." Paste over it another sticker, one that says "I Make Smart Choices."

To make the change, we must replace our old way of thinking. It is not easy cutting back on the hectic life. We have grown accustomed to the excitement and may even be hooked on the adrenaline surge we get from it. Although the price we must pay for this new way of thinking seems high, the results are worth it. Here's how it's done.

1. **Lead an evenly paced life according to your personal rhythm.** Find your best rhythm and stick to it. I am an early morning person. I go to bed about nine o'clock every night and wake up about quarter after five every morning. I don't

deviate very much from this routine. Sometimes I must stay up later. On a really wild night, I may go entirely berserk and stay up as late as eleven. But I pay for it the next day, and as soon as possible I get back into my routine.

In *Body Rhythm: The Circadian Rhythms within You*, author Lee Weston tells of studies showing that if we get too far out of our natural circadian rhythm, we bring stress into our lives, resulting in physical problems. People who lead stressful lives can't deviate as much from their regular schedule as those who live less pressured lives.

Everyone's rhythm cycle is different, but if you find yours and stick to it, you will be stronger than if you're always wasting energy fighting your own body.

2. **Make time for things that bring emotional support.** Ever since women stopped living in large family groups, drawing water together at the communal well, and doing laundry in the creek as a group, we have lived isolated and often lonely lives. Women need support. To do without it is detrimental.

Take relationships such as friendships seriously. Make time to keep them up. Find supportive groups. It may be a church group. Church involvement gives people many supporters that help alleviate stress. It may be a self-help group such as a Messies Anonymous group—either one in your area or on the www.messies.com website.

What inspires me may not inspire you. Search your soul to find out what encourages you. For instance, if great literature thrills you, you may wish to go back to college and study it.

3. **Replace negative thoughts with positive ones.** Don't dwell on bad news in the paper. Don't ponder problems on the television news. Avoid people who are fascinated by bad news and negative thoughts. We are the first people in history to know within minutes about a tragedy on the other side of the world. In colonial days it took weeks before the country knew who had been elected president. Now we know before the election is over. Bad news travels just as fast. We gather

more bad news in a day than the pioneers knew from the outside world in a year. The human spirit can take only so much news about murders, hijackings, floods, and terrorism without being distressed by the enormity of it all. How many people can we see carried out on gurneys, crying over loved ones trapped under earthquake debris, or —well, you get the idea. Our minds were not built to absorb this much tragedy on a day-to-day basis. All of this bad news is further frustrating because we are powerless to do anything about it.

In the place of bad news, read uplifting books. In the morning when I get up, I have about a half hour alone when I can pray and read the Bible or another book that fortifies me for the day. In the Bible Paul gives some instructions that have special benefit in our modern stressful world:

> Finally brethren, whatever things are true, whatever things are noble, whatever things are just, whatever things are pure, whatever things are lovely, whatever things are of good report, if there is any virtue and if there is anything praiseworthy—meditate on these things.
>
> Philippians 4:8 NKJV

4. **Avoid conflicts.** We can't always avoid conflicts, but some people are careless about getting into them. They seem unable to understand how they constantly bring conflicts into their own lives. Some conflicts, of course, can be avoided only by removing ourselves entirely from the person or situation involved.

If the conflict causes you to become upset or excited, the adrenal glands and several others begin to work overtime preparing the body for fight or flight. Since it is unlikely that you will either get in a fight or run away, your body will simply be revved up and stressed out for nothing.

Indecision is another form of conflict. Messies have a lot of that. Since we are perfectionists and always want to make the right decision, we spend a lot of time and energy wrestling with each choice. Wrestling is exhausting. And we do it over every little thing. When I first began to get rid of excess possessions, I could only do it for an hour or so a day because the decision making wore me out. I wanted to keep things, but I knew I could not live the way I wanted to with so much stuff in my house. I was under a lot of pressure, and my body felt it.

In her book *Women and Fatigue*, Holly Atkinson says, "Conflicts . . . are a major source of fatigue in women. Such conscious or unconscious struggles between two opposing desires or courses of action keep the brain working overtime, which uses more energy."

5. **Assume proper leadership.** Take the role of the authoritative person you ought to be. If your attitude is passive and pliable, others will control your life and you will be frustrated, stressed, and tired. But if you have confidence that your thoughts, desires, and plans are worthwhile and productive, it will show in the way you stand, speak, and conduct yourself. People will respect you and your plans. You will not always be right, but you will be in control. This will relieve the stress of helplessness.

As you change from being passive to assertive, those around you will go through four stages of adjustment. Our country went through these stages when faced with the civil rights movement and the Vietnam protests. They were also the stages the church went through in the first century. So don't take it personally when you see it happening to you.

In the beginning, they will ignore you. They will hope this is just a phase that will go away if they pretend it is unimportant.

Then they will misinterpret it. They will say, "Mother is just not herself lately. Perhaps it is that time of month," or "She's on another one of her improvement kicks." They will say anything except "Mother wants things to be different, and she is certainly right."

Still later, when they see that you won't back down, they will resist your desires with a certain sense of urgency. They will attack you for not letting things rock along as they have been. You may hear such statements as, "You are making a nuisance of yourself." "I will pick those things up in a little while." "Don't be such a grouch." "I wish you were the way you used to be." When this happens, just say to yourself, "Stage three."

Finally, when they see that all these approaches do not deter you, they will begin the final stage, cooperation, and you and they will be the better for it.

For more information on how to accomplish assuming leadership, check out the books *When You Live with a Messie*, which relates to husbands, and *Neat Mom, Messy Kids*.

6. **Control your stressors.** Become proficient in what you do. If housekeeping is one of your big stressors, figure out what to do and how to do it. Get to the point where your house is under control because you are more powerful than it is. Your house, which up to this time has frustrated and humiliated you, is no longer a source of stress because you have found a stronger force—the power of ability. Just knowing you can control it helps relieve tension. The real tension will be relieved when the house is beautiful and orderly. Then the stress of an ugly house, so powerful because it is so closely tied to womanhood, will be alleviated.

Peruse your bookstore or library for a book on organizing that speaks your language. *The Messies Manual* is designed to give you guidance on getting control of your house and staying in control.

I would be remiss if I didn't mention that perhaps there are other areas you should begin thinking of changing as well. Stressors are multiple. Some are out of our control. Many are not. Take steps to control these other stress areas as well.

7. **Remember your body.** Exercise is the greatest stress reliever. Such activities as walking, biking, and yoga get the blood flowing and the body moving to ease out the knots of stress. When the heart starts to pump and the lungs start to pull in good clean air, the mind begins to see things more clearly. Life looks better. Sleep comes more easily.

Tension usually affects the head and neck, so the following exercises focus on those areas. And most of them are stretching exercises, since muscles begin to shorten as they are tensed by stress. You can do them while sitting down. Most of them can be done in public places without fear of looking weird. Some you can do in your car, but home is always a good place.

The feeling of helplessness in controlling one's life is a major source of stress.

a. *The Neck Roll.* Bend your head forward as though nibbling the button off your blouse. Then roll your head over to your shoulder, forward again, to the other shoulder, and back to the front. Repeat several times. (A more familiar version of this exercise is to roll your head toward your back, but recent medical studies have shown that this is unhealthy.)

b. *The Shoulder Shrug.* Hunch your shoulders up as high as you can toward your ears, as though you were indicating "I don't know." Rotate them forward, down, back, and up again. Do this two or three times in both directions.

c. *The Big Hug.* Hold your arms out to the sides parallel to the floor. Keeping your arms as high as possible while standing straight, touch your hands together behind you. Now bring them forward across your body to your shoulders and give yourself a big hug. Even if the stretch doesn't work wonders, the hug will.

d. *The Stretch.* Lift your hands high over your head as though reaching for something. Keep them there for a few seconds. Lower them. Then do the same with one hand at a time. Do this until you feel relief in the back and shoulders.

e. *Massage.* Take time to gently massage your neck and shoulders, rubbing in circles on those tight muscles until they begin to soften a little.

f. *A warm tub filled with bubble bath.* Soaking in a candlelit bathroom can do wonders. A friend with whom I shared this idea said she is going broke buying candles and bubble bath because she likes it so much.

g. *A professional massage and hot tub.* If they're available, this combination can also do the trick, but most of us will have to settle for a simple bubble bath.

Finding Balance

We do not want to lead stress-free lives. Nothing is as boring as a do-nothing life that is so unchallenging that we become flaccid. We need to find some cause or goal that encourages us to strive for excellence in some area.

Stress that is out of control weakens our lives. We become angry. We can't function well. We need to be strong, capable women to fulfill the plan for which we were put into the world. Facing what is within our control, we need to be willing to make the necessary changes.

Ten Suggestions for Beating Stress

(I would call them commandments but I am not God, and besides, commandments might add to your stress.)

1. Accept your own imperfections and go ahead in spite of them.
2. Avoid fighting for anything that is not really worth it. Don't squander your energy on semi-important things.
3. Learn and follow organizing principles.
4. Say "no" more often.
5. Get rid of a lot.
6. Don't gather much.
7. Don't keep much.
8. Value simplicity in your lifestyle.
9. Don't sweat the little things. (Everything—well, almost everything—is a little thing.)
10. Be grateful.

Assess the Mess

1. List your biggest sources of stress.

    a.

    b.

    c.

2. Which of the ten suggestions will you use to help you overcome this stress?

    a.

    b.

    c.

16

learning from your friends

Tigger, our cat, had not been well, so we took him to the vet. My husband wanted to carry Tigger in a cage, but I assured him I could handle the cat with no problem. Tigger rode quietly in my lap all the way to the vet's office, which is located on one of the busiest streets in Miami. Many cars that regularly drive on it wear bumper stickers with the slogan "Pray for me. I drive on Bird Road." We knew we had to be careful getting the cat out of the car and into the vet's office. We parked as close to the door as possible. As soon as my husband opened the door on my side of the car and I stood up with the cat in my arms, our placid, cooperative animal became a maniac. Scratching my arms and using his back legs to push off, the cat flailed in all directions. My husband and I were flailing too, afraid to let go of the cat and afraid to hold him. Both of us tried to hold on to some part. Finally the cat was on the ground between two parked cars, and one of us, I don't remember which one, had hold of the frantic, fighting animal by only one foot. Our worst fears were about to come true.

In the midst of the melee, I saw a streak of white, and the cat disappeared. When I gained my composure, I saw a young man in a long white lab coat standing on the sidewalk in front of the car holding an unhappy but very controlled cat in his arms. He was the vet's assistant.

I asked him later where he had come from. He had just stepped out of the office to help another owner carry his pet's cage to the car. He had seen our plight. The rest was obvious.

"All you have to do is hold him like this right on the back of his neck," he said, demonstrating. He was right. You just had to know how.

Like Tigger, our houses get totally out of control sometimes. We think we can handle it alone, but despite our confidence and best plans, we can't.

At these times we need to bring in professional help—either a book or a professional organizer who will come to our home, grab our whirlwind by the scruff of the neck, and say, "Here's how."

Sometimes we don't have to go far. We can learn from our friends and neighbors who have orderly homes but don't seem to work at it.

Every quantifiable aspect of life can be divided into three parts: height can be divided into short, average, and tall; weight into skinny, average, and fat; the way we eat into anorexic, normal, and overeater. In the same way, housekeeping skills can be divided into Messie, Average, and Cleanie. Like the anorexic and overeater who both have an eating problem, Cleanies and Messies both have a cleaning problem. Both have a compulsion to control things.

The Cleanie is visually sensitive. She wants to have visual things under her control. She cannot stand the sight of clutter or dirt. Everything has its place, usually out of sight, and she makes sure it stays there so she can find it when she wants it. Her area of responsibility is narrow and well-defined. She works hard and long. She keeps a tight rein on her household. This puts great stress on her family because living in such a house is never relaxing.

The Messie also wishes to be in control, but she takes a different approach. She keeps everything in sight so she will have it when she needs it. She keeps a lot of things she is unlikely to need because, as she says, "You never know. Someone might need it someday." This great bulk of material, much of it sitting out so she can keep an eye on it, is a great distress to her family and to herself as well. The house is not pleasant to live in, and it does not look good. Nobody can find things, the house is hard to clean, and the family is embarrassed to invite people over. The Messie feels as if she works hard all the time but accomplishes little.

The average housekeeper does not have a housekeeping problem. She blithely goes along with a pleasant house. She takes pride and pleasure in her house, but she doesn't work at housekeeping very much. Frazzled Messies wonder when she does it. She seems to spend her hours doing pleasant things, such as having coffee with friends or going out. The pleasant house is important to her. The housekeeping is not. She knows she is not perfect, and she is comfortable with that fact. She is average, but she is successful.

That is what we are going to aim for—to be a successful average housekeeper. We do not want to trade being a Messie for being a Cleanie any more than an overweight person wants to trade overeating for anorexia.

MESSIE	AVERAGE	CLEANIE
1	5	10

Put an arrow at the point where you are now. Then draw a stick figure where you wish to be. Put a smiley face on the figure. Think of how nice it will be to live that kind of life.

To find out how successful average housekeepers keep their houses nice without much effort, I interviewed some women I had known for several years. To determine if they were successful average housekeepers, I used two criteria: (1) Over a period of years were their houses consistently in good order when I visited, with or without prior notice? (2) Did they show a marked disinterest in housekeeping?

When I interviewed Cleanies for a previous book, *The Messies Manual*, I thought they seemed rather detached about housekeeping. But once I got them going, they began to tell me their schedules, attitudes, tricks, and techniques, which were legion.

You just have to know how to do it.

In contrast, the successful average housekeepers I interviewed never really warmed up to the subject. They downgraded the importance of the whole thing. Housekeeping was not their number one priority. They were consistent in saying they liked to have a nice house, but they were also consistently casual about how they accomplished it. When pushed they said they cleaned routinely. "I just do it to get it done," said one. "It's just a routine, you know," said another. One said she enjoyed cleaning. Another said she liked her house, and she enjoyed taking care of it. They did not spend much time doing housework. Perhaps five hours a week to clean and organize closets, cupboards, and so on. I told one woman that I had heard of someone who could clean her house in two hours a week. Apparently unimpressed and distracted by the party she was hosting at the time, she mumbled, "Forty-five minutes would be more like it."

I interviewed women from many circumstances—from a retiree who lived alone in a three bedroom house to a woman who worked part time and lived with five people from three generations in the same size house as the single retiree. The women I interviewed all lived in South Florida, where the houses are small and the yards large because people spend more time outside. But their attitudes apply universally.

1. **Successful housekeepers want their houses to look nice.** They do not keep a nice house so it will work well, so they find things, or so they can store things. Repeatedly they say they want the house to look good.

Messies usually focus on the house working well. At one seminar I asked the participants why they wanted to get their houses in order. All who answered gave practical reasons: "So I can find things," "So I won't be embarrassed," "So I can get my kids off to school without so much hassle," and "So I won't have to work so hard." One woman timidly raised her hand and asked, "Would it be all right to say I want my house to look nice?"

That was what I was waiting for! Her answer hit the heart of the reason successful average housekeepers keep the house nice. People who want their houses to look nice end up having houses that work well, and people who want their houses to work well end up with houses that don't work or look nice. The reason for this is that the emotional response to beauty is more powerful than practicality. A captivating vision of a lovely home will pull a reforming Messie much further along than the urge to have a working home.

2. **Successful housekeepers are nice to themselves.** They believe they deserve a nice house and that it is okay for them to have what they need and want. They do not deny themselves as Messies do. They may go without something because they do not have the money to get it, but they do not do it out of principle.

3. **Successful housekeepers trust their feelings.** They have good instincts about what to keep and what to get rid of. They are a great deal more casual than Messies when it comes to things in the house. They do not *love* things the way Messies do. They do not *fear* making a mistake, not having an important item, or giving away something they will want later.

What really amazed me when I was talking to them was their relationships to their collections. One had a collection of clown figurines and pictures. As I looked around her house, I saw that the shelf of clown figurines seemed to be full. "What will you do with other figurines you may get?" I asked. "I've stopped collecting them," she replied. I was amazed. I didn't know you could stop a collection when you ran out of space. I thought a collection was like a friendship. You kept it up even if it became inconvenient.

Like the anorexic and overeater who both have an eating problem, Cleanies and Messies both have a cleaning problem.

Another woman who had a collection of blue glass said the same thing. She was about to stop collecting it because her window ledge was filling up.

They also have casual feelings about books and magazines. Those who love and receive magazines regularly enjoy reading them and sharing them with friends. They keep them as long as they wish and then throw them away or take them to the Laundromat, beauty parlor, or a neighbor.

When I asked these successful average housekeepers if they kept the bottom portion of bills after paying them (the part that says "Keep this portion for your own records") some did but most did not. They said the canceled check was enough. This was amazing to me since the stub says very clearly what to do with it. I have always been happy to keep the stubs and probably would have kept them even if I'd never been instructed to do so. These are cavalier people who live dangerously. I'll bet they even remove the tag from pillows that says "Do not remove under penalty of law."

On the other hand, they keep whatever they want and buy whatever they need, within the limits of their finances of course. This freedom spares them from the sense of impending deprivation that makes Messies want to keep everything.

The book of Proverbs has an interesting comment on this phenomenon: "It is possible to give away and become richer!

It is also possible to hold on too tightly and lose everything. Yes, the liberal man shall be rich! By watering others, he waters himself" (11:24–25 TLB).

Is this not true of the situation we are describing? Those who willingly give things away gain a beautiful, orderly house. Those who hold on to everything lose what they are hoarding, the peace and comfort of ownership.

The point I am making is that successful average housekeepers are not driven by their emotions in such a way that love or fear binds them to keep something. They are emotionally detached, whether keeping or buying. This detachment gives them the freedom to decide wisely.

Two successful average housekeepers I interviewed stressed the importance of moderation. One said, "I do things in moderation. I don't want to be a fanatic. It makes a person too tense." The other said, "Moderation is the key word with everything."

4. **Successful housekeepers are alert to the house.** They know when it is cluttered, full, empty, pretty, and so on. Unlike the Messie, the successful housekeeper has a feel for the condition of the house. It is similar to hunger and fullness. People who overeat are often unaware of when they are hungry or full, so they eat inappropriately. A normal person eats when hungry and stops when full. The overweight person eats out of habit, without thought of hunger, without tasting her food. The normal person is aware of the taste and amount of food she takes in.

In a similar way, Messies function as machines when it comes to the house. They do many destructive things without realizing the negative impact they will have. The mail is a good example. Messies frequently put it in a pile on a table with little thought or care. They keep it, junk and all, as a matter of course. They also keep receipts and coupons mindlessly.

Here are some techniques to help you decide what to keep until you break the "keep everything" habit.

a. *Be aware of the things happening in the house.* When you want to buy something, especially something big, do not do so until you know where to put it. For a day or two before you buy it, visualize where it will go and how it will fit in.

b. *Rate the things you're not sure whether or not you should keep.* Pick a closet or a drawer and sort everything in it into three piles. If you really want or need something, put it in pile one and put it neatly where it belongs when you finish this exercise. If you are ambivalent about something, put it in pile two, store it in an ambivalence box, and put today's date on it. Whatever you don't use in the next month, get rid of. Put the things you don't need into pile three and give them to a good cause or throw them away.

> "It is possible to give away and become richer! It is also possible to hold on too tightly and lose everything."

When saving becomes a conscious decision rather than an automatic reflex, your house will have a lot less clutter. If while cleaning the closet you find a piece of clothing you don't like at all, put it in pile three and get rid of it. If you're going through your mail drawer and find an advertisement about rifles and you've never hunted in your life, put it in pile three. If you're saving it for a friend who hunts, address an envelope to him and put it in the mail. Or better yet, discard it immediately. Do not set it down again.

The condition of your house depends on your ability to make decisions about your clutter. A decision delayed is a decision unmade, and a decision unmade lets clutter invade.

In the past you kept things because you had a vague feeling they might be good for something someday. You were an automatic saving machine. Now the automatic part has been turned off and you have taken control of what you keep and what you get rid of.

5. **Successful housekeepers live in the present.** This characteristic has broad implications. Because they do not live in, think about, or worry much about the past, they do not keep much memorabilia, including receipts, stubs, or old trophies.

Not one person I interviewed had a file cabinet. All of them had a small drawer for their papers. One kept insisting that she did have a file. It was a little accordion-style divider folder about the size of a business envelope. In it she kept all her important papers and her records about bills. She could hold it in her hand, and she kept it in a drawer. One woman had a box at a bank where she kept such things as birth certificates and mortgages.

The reason Messies are more likely to have big file cabinets may be symbolic. File cabinets symbolize order, and Messies, recognizing their need for this elusive quality, probably figure "the bigger the better." So they buy a big file cabinet and wait for it to organize their lives. Instead, it becomes another place of disorder. It may be a slight improvement. Now the papers are all in one place. But even that advantage is debatable because sometimes it's easier to find papers among books, magazines, and newspapers than it is to find a particular paper among an array of similar looking papers.

Another advantage of living in the present is not always having to plan for the future. I was amazed at how these women did projects without long-range planning. One had just redone her bathroom. It was absolutely breathtaking with black tub, toilet, and sink, light gray tile, and lots of mirrors. I asked her how they had planned it. Had they looked at a lot of magazines on bathrooms? Had they shopped a lot for the best prices? Had they received professional advice?

No, they had gone to a showroom, gotten their brochure, and called to ask the prices of the items they selected. They had them installed by a carpenter who had no opinions and offered no advice but loved the bathroom when it was finished. They did not have a file full of ideas before they began. They did not plan long ahead.

This lack of long-range planning—for hobbies, travel, decorating, or whatever—was consistent among successful average housekeepers. When they wanted to do something, they knew where to find the necessary information. A number of them had just remodeled their homes. They all did it the same way—by going to a few stores until they saw what they liked. They all seemed happy with their choices.

Messies, on the other hand, frequently have many big projects on the burner for some time in the undetermined future. They hoard brochures and magazines, fearing that when the time comes to do the project they will not know what they want or where to get it. I believe some Messies overplan because they don't think they will ever accomplish their plans. Collecting things is a subconscious wish to participate in what they do not really expect will happen. In the end, the Messies who plan so diligently are frequently less successful than those who do not plan much at all.

Successful average housekeepers are not particularly fearful. They do not worry that some forgetfulness from the past will come back to haunt them. They are confident of their own tastes. They don't have a lot of partially finished projects lying around, so they don't fear starting new ones. They do not fear the future, so they don't keep things they may need someday.

6. **Successful housekeepers work with detachment.** They don't wait until they feel like doing the job. This does not seem to occur to them. Instead, they shift into an automatic mode of moving the body through certain routines they have established and do on a regular basis. As they do this regularly, before they know it, the house is in good shape. The approach they use saves the energy we waste in decision making and emotional involvement. It is probably one of the chief differences between those who are consistently successful and those who are not.

The moral of this story is this: do yourself a favor and get a routine. Make a schedule for morning, evening, and various points during the day. Follow it consistently without even thinking about it. While you are wondering how it is happening, your house will change slowly but surely before your eyes.

The Successful Average Housekeeper Mentality

It is not enough for us to see what successful average house-keepers do; we must catch the feeling of how they think. They are optimistic and fearless when it comes to housekeeping. They are confident of their own tastes and power over the house. They live in the present and do not hang on to the past. Their lives are so fulfilling that they are not afraid of being shortchanged.

In *Diets Don't Work*, author Bob Schwartz suggests that his readers approach food the way a thin person does. We can take a clue from this exercise and learn to approach our belongings the way a successful average housekeeper does, using that same optimism, detachment, resolve, and desire.

Changing is like being a trapeze artist. She swings into midair holding a bar. Back and forth she swings, higher and higher. As soon as she gets high enough, she lets go of the bar and catches one coming from the opposite direction. To get to the other bar she must let go of the first. This is the way it is when you let go of the old way of thinking. Making the change is scary, but if you want to get to the new bar, you have to let go of the old one.

Assess the Mess

1. These are my worst fears about what would happen if I detached myself from the things in my house:

   a.
   b.
   c.
   d.

2. These are the activities I would like to change in my life (e.g., I would stop magazine subscriptions):

I would stop

I would start

3. Some of the things that detract from the beauty of my home are:

   a.
   b.
   c.
   d.

4. The thinking patterns I need to let go of are:

   a.
   b.
   c.
   d.

5. The thinking patterns I need to take hold of are:

   a.
   b.
   c.
   d.

Perhaps you think you could profit from hiring a professional organizer to zero in on how you can improve the organization of your home. I want to point out, however, that the real problem is not your house; it's your mind-set. Until that is changed, there will be no permanent change in your house, no matter how many professionals you hire. If professional organizers get your house in perfect order before you change your mind-set, the house will slip back into its former condition.

Professional organizers can be a significant part of the change you are making. They may help you know how to begin, or they may step in when you get as far as you can on your own. To find a professional organizer in your area, contact the National Association of Professional Organizers (www.NAPO.net). Ask to be directed to someone who works in the area of chronic disorganization. The Professional Organizers' Web Ring (www.organizerswebring.com) offers organizing articles, products, and a directory of professional organizers.

17

getting the family to help

Messies have varying home backgrounds as far as house-keeping is concerned. Some had meticulous mothers who kept the house in order at all times. Housekeeping was both their hobby and career. The little Messie child came into this orderly world and neither Mom nor Messie could figure out what was happening. The child and the mom were in repeated conflict. Mom won most of the time. Sometimes the child grew up hating the thing that caused so much of her childhood trouble—that superorderly house.

Some had moms who were Messies too. Messie mom and Messie child had a tough time fighting the house together, and sometimes each blamed the other for being the source of the trouble. In desperation Mom would look to the child to help more than any child, especially a Messie child, could. This Messie child also grew up hating the house, the source of conflict and embarrassment.

Most Messies were probably brought up in an average household where the mom was confident of her own ability to keep things under control and didn't make a big thing of it. She was flexible, but only to a point. The little Messie grew up with her mess controlled but without being unduly pressured about the house. She may not have realized the extent of her messy problem. This is the child who is surprised that housekeeping is hard for her. Mom never made a big deal of it, and everything was fine. But when she doesn't make a big deal over keeping house, the whole thing goes to pot.

> You are not searching for perfection. You do not want to turn into a nag who makes coming home miserable.

Your Family Now

A recovering Messie needs the help of the family to solve the problem of an out-of-control house. You need them to support you in the change you are making. You also need them to cooperate with you in your plans. The first is negotiable; the second, within limits, is not.

Support

You may have a number of personal relationships to consider when you think about your family and the house. Whatever their opinions about the change in your life, you need to talk clearly to them about the support you want. They may or may not be sympathetic. If they are, that is a help for you. If they are not, you will continue with your change and perhaps later they will understand and offer their support.

There are four reasons why the family of the Messie may resist the change. First, some spouses subconsciously resist because they are used to being superior in regard to the house. They have gotten into the habit of fussing at the Messie and telling her what to do around the house. When the Messie begins to take control, that area of dominance begins to disappear, and the husband may resent it.

Second, some spouses feel as if they have lost a trump card in the relationship. If the husband used the messiness of the house as an excuse for requiring other things from his wife to compensate, he will no longer be able to demand these "extras."

Third, the husband himself may have been using the condition of the house as an excuse for not doing certain things, such as entertaining.

Fourth, the husband may have been blaming his wife for the total problem of messiness. If she changes, it will become obvious that he and other members of the family are not innocent victims of Mom's problem.

Keep these reasons for resistance in mind when you explain to your family your need for their support. Frequently they are not aware of their own resistance. Ask clearly for their support and together work through the problems that arise.

Cooperation

The area of cooperation is not negotiable. Your family will have to do their part in the house. Care must be taken here. You are not searching for perfection. You do not want to turn into a nag who makes coming home miserable. When you make changes in what you expect from them, they will have some long-established habits to break.

You may also have a dyed-in-the-wool Messie child who is afraid to change, afraid to get rid of his or her personal clutter. When you are working against this compulsive fear, you need to be understanding—but firm.

Successful average housekeepers expect their families to cooperate and, in most cases, people do what is expected of them. One of the successful average housekeepers I spoke to had three rules for her family:

1. Remove your dirty dishes from the table, rinse them, and put them in the dishwasher.
2. Put your dirty clothes and towels in the hamper.
3. Wipe the shower wall after a shower (a must).

From time to time she asks them to do a few other jobs, like folding clothes from the dryer or unloading the dishwasher. Her opinion is that if they know they are going to be part of cleaning up, they will be more careful about messing up, and they will share more fully in the pride of having a lovely home.

Stop Playing the Game

So far this chapter has been pretty straightforward, suggesting that you understand your situation, set firm goals, and insist that they cooperate. In many cases that is enough. A firm consistent adherence to your goal will undoubtedly go far.

But sometimes, or maybe often, things don't flow easily in the right direction. The book *Neat Mom, Messie Kids* deals in detail with the issues involved in this complicated managerial endeavor.

One of the reasons changing family behavior is difficult is that household tasks are often part of a larger game the family plays. Each player is working himself or herself to death to be a winner. Because it has been going on for a long time and is subtle, the players don't realize they have chosen sides and set up rigid rules. The goals vary. Sometimes it solidifies family relationships in ways that are too complex to mention here. The result is that Mom is unhappy about the cooperation she gets, and the other members of the family feel some satisfaction about the way things are going.

There are many solutions that might work. One way is to dismantle the game altogether by refusing to play by the already established rules. When one person, especially an important player such as Mom, stops playing the game, it cannot continue.

Husband as Player

Let us look at one of the roles a husband might play. There might be households in which the husband takes charge of the household and directs the work of the resisting wife. While husbands have their own area of leadership, for better or worse, managing the household falls to the woman. Ordinarily, a woman would respond by explaining why going this route is not a good setup for her or the house. She resists and attempts to establish the organizing of the house as her territory. His dominance and her resistance are the way they have decided to play the game.

A possible solution is to dismantle the rules of the game by suggesting that he take over the direction of the household and give her more instruction as to exactly how he wants things done. She may ask him to write it down clearly, to schedule minutely. This may be a disaster in some cases. In others it may so shift the balance of power that it dismantles the "I'm in charge, you are resisting" game on which that part of the relationship is built, because he will not want to officially direct.

The Child as Player

Children are masterful game players. They can have you in the middle of an all-out championship contest, and you will hardly know you are playing. You will just be confused and frustrated. If you step out of the game, it will not continue. Here are some examples that will shock some conscientious and kindly parents. But changing the rules of the game may be the kindest thing you can do for your children.

• Your child drops her book bag beside the front door every day. You fuss every day, but nothing changes. You tell her that next time she does it you are going to throw it out in the front yard. She leaves it there the next day because that is the way the game has always been played. She waits for your chiding. When she can't find the bag to do her work, you tell her that it is where you told her it would be. If she even remembers what you said, she will be shocked to find it in the front yard. Leaving it by the front door will no longer be a winning move for her.

• You have been asking your child to put his dirty clothes into the clothes hamper. Simple enough, right? But he seems to walk off leaving his things on the floor just beside the hamper. You make your statement. "Son, from now on I will wash only the clothes that I take out of the hamper." To follow it up, any time clothes are left on the floor, you kick them under the bed or to the back of the closet. If that placement does not seem to be convenient for you, bag them in some out-of-the-way place. When he runs out of clothes or the ones he likes, point out where they are. Now he may handle the problem in whatever way seems best to him. You will not be involved in washing them at this point.

There are many variations on how to handle the laundry issue. Kids should be doing their own, and perhaps family laundry, early on in life. The point is, however you do it, you set the rules of the game in a way in which bad behavior automatically impacts negatively on him. Conversely, good behavior impacts positively. In this way, everybody is a winner in the long term. It is certainly fairer than the way the game used to be played.

Personalities of the Game Players

The game-changing solution is not for everybody. Some sincere souls will feel very uncomfortable with viewing family relationships in a game metaphor. If you feel this approach is disrespectful of family values and members, then you need to try other more straightforward approaches more in keeping with your core beliefs. Or perhaps you feel that the personalities of your family members do not lend themselves to this approach. You know your family best. After all, our desire is to strengthen the family in an overall way, not cause unnecessary problems.

However, for some this approach will make a world of sense. "Ah, ha!" you may say, "I see it all now! Of course! We have all been unwittingly playing a very destructive game with each other. This is an easy way to change things without having a big to-do about it."

It works well for those who appreciate the idea. They think it is a hoot to concoct imaginative new rules for a better game. They are prepared for the family reaction and stay pretty much one step ahead of them. Anyone trying this method can surely expect a strong negative reaction. That indicates that change is about to take place. When it is rightly done, rather rapid change takes place and the family moves forward, strengthened by the whole affair.

Consider Shakespeare and the Martial Arts

Literary-minded folks will recognize the game-changing approach as the one taken by Petruchio with his difficult wife, Katherina, in Shakespeare's *Taming of the Shrew*. No one wanted to marry Katherina because she was such an unpleasant complainer.

In order to "tame" her, Petruchio did not try to stop her complaining. Instead, he took her complaining much more seriously than she intended. When poorly prepared food arrived, he sent it away and they went hungry. When it seemed that the bed was not made properly, he did not let either of them sleep on it. Because of his behavior, the difficult Katherina was put in the position of defending the servants and asking for patience and forgiveness. She changed. Petruchio's approach turned out well for him—and the now-changed Katherina. You decide if you want to follow the bard's system.

In a similar vein, those who know the martial arts recall that sometimes it is best not to take the direct approach of resistance. Judo teaches to use the opponent's forward motion and pull the opponent further forward. Aikido similarly teaches to go with the energy of the attacker and redirect his energy. Sometimes, resistance is not the best approach.

Applying the System

As a further illustration, think about the problem of picking up the bathroom after bathing. Let us say you have cajoled, begged, threatened, and maybe punished those who walk out leaving towels and clothes on the floor. The situation you face is that they have left them in the wrong place. How can you practice nonresistance and escalate the problem further in the direction the individual is already going? Without speaking to the messer, you move the towels and clothes into an even more incorrect place by putting them in a plastic bag and storing them out of the way. You are not striving to put them in the correct place, such as on the towel rack or in the dirty clothes hamper. Instead, you are taking the misplacement to a higher level. The person who needs the towel or clothes in the future may certainly retrieve them out of the closet, garage, or basement if they wish. Let us hope for his or her sake they have not become mildewed. Perhaps the person will decide it is wiser to immediately retrieve them off of the bathroom floor next time. As always, the choice belongs to the individual.

The family is definitely not a shrew to be tamed or an enemy to be defeated. However, these parallels help us visualize how to use nonresistance to help those who have developed poor organizational skills change for the better.

Assess the Mess

1. Who will you need to talk to about supporting your change?
   a.
   b.
   c.
   d.
   e.

2. When will you talk to each of them?

3. What strategy will you use to convince them of the importance of their cooperation?

4. List the names of people whose cooperation you need for success. Beside their names, write the tasks you want them to do or improvements you want them to make.

Names	Tasks You Want Them to Do
1.	
2.	
3.	

5. If you decide to use the game-changing idea, list the areas in which you need to change your approach. Try only one or two at a time. Continue as you see need after one area is changed.

Family Behavior to Change	My New Reaction
1.	
2.	
3.	

18

doing nice things for yourself

Former President Reagan's daughter, Maureen, and I agreed in a telephone interview that we did not make any improvement in the house if it required more than five minutes and more than a hammer to do. I mention this conversation because I like to drop famous names wherever possible. You may know this if you read my third book, *The Messies Superguide*, in which I was even able to work in the name of the Queen of England in relation to Messies Anonymous.

I also mention it to introduce the kind of helpful hints you will find in my books. Most of them are simple to do. It is not that I disapprove of others that are complicated; I just don't do them. At the end of this chapter, I will mention books with suggestions that require more extensive use of time and tools. I am not very handy with tools, but I am better than my husband. When work needs to be done around the house, I hire a local handyman. My husband doesn't mind if someone else does the job, though he prefers to be out of town when it's done. I found this out from experience.

Most of the suggestions I make here are easy and quick to do.

The Telephone Area

Did you ever hear a frustrated voice at the other end of the telephone line saying, "Just a minute. This pen doesn't work. The pen at my phone never works. Phil, will you hand me that pen! Just a minute. Phil, my pen doesn't work! Hand me a pen or a pencil! Okay. Okay. Now I'm ready. Go ahead."

Perhaps you were the frustrated voice at the end of the line. And once you found a pen, where did you write the message? And where did you put the message after writing it? The telephone message center is often one of the most confused areas in the disorganized household, and it is one of the easiest to get organized. Do yourself a favor and organize your phone center. You need only a few basic items.

The first is the aforementioned pen. Buy one that sticks to the side of the phone with a coiled wire or chain. That way no one can pick it up and take it away "for just a minute" and fail to return it. Frequently you can find a pen to coordinate with the phone color. Look in a variety store, an office supply store, or a drugstore.

The second piece of equipment you need is a spiral-bound notebook designed to take phone messages and record them in duplicate. The one I have will hold four hundred messages. The top copy tears out, and the duplicate stays in the book. If someone calls and leaves a phone number for your husband, you write it in the book, tear out the top paper, and give it to him. If he loses it, you still have a record of it. You will be surprised at how often you refer to your permanent record. Keep this record book near the phone.

The third piece of equipment to buy is an address file. The Rolodex type system I have comes in two sizes. I use the larger size, three-by-five inch, because I put more than just telephone numbers and addresses on it. The one I use has no cover because taking it off is just one more hindrance to using the system easily. Mine sits right on top of the phone table.

The fourth piece of equipment you'll need is a telephone table to put the phone on or to put under the wall phone. Don't try to make do without adequate storage space at the phone. This is particularly important for people who live in cities where there is more than one large phone book to contend with. Look for a phone table at odd places. Furniture stores may have them. I ordered mine from a mail-order catalog. The phone books and spiral-bound message book go in it.

Phones have come a long way, baby. Time was when we were anchored to the wall and could only use longer cords to get some freedom from the base of the phone. Now, of course, cordless and cell phones have solved the problem. Headsets that work in conjunction with both cordless and corded phones free up our hands in addition to giving us roaming room while we are talking.

Some people can wash dishes, dust, and do complex work while they talk. Others can't. One of the successful average housekeepers I talked to always picks up a damp cloth when she is on the phone and begins to wipe her kitchen. During long conversations she polishes her brass things. Usually I use talking time as a time to sit down and rest.

Take full advantage of answering machines, Caller ID, and all of the present and developing technology that you determine will make life easier and more productive. Be nice to yourself. Make your phone arrangements more convenient for you and your family.

The Kitchen Area

The main thing to be done to the kitchen is to unclutter it. By looking at things piece by piece, we will be able to get the kitchen under control and in easy working order.

First of all, let's face it. The real problem in the kitchen is way, way, way too much junk. Some of it was given to us by older women who should have known we'd never use it. Some we bought ourselves when we were young and foolish and thought we would need it. Some we bought when we were old and foolish. Women are suckers for anything that promises to make us better nurturers. That's why it is so hard to get rid of kitchen things. But the more junk we keep, the less effective our nurturing will be. It gives an illusion of nurturing but little of the reality.

Pack in boxes things you have not used for a while. On the boxes write a date about two months from when you pack it. You can retrieve things from the boxes until that date. Whatever you haven't retrieved by then, give to charity.

> The more junk we keep, the less effective our nurturing will be. It gives an illusion of nurturing but little of the reality.

Countertops

The countertop sets the stage for the atmosphere of the kitchen. If it is neat, the whole kitchen looks neat. To clear the countertop, look for ways to get as much off it as possible.

Under-the-counter appliances—such as coffeemakers, can openers, toasters, broiler ovens, radios and televisions, microwave ovens, hand mixers, and blenders—are a great help in recovering lost counter space. Almost all small appliances can now be removed from valuable countertops. You must, however, make careful decisions as to what appliances to purchase for that purpose. After all, under-the-counter space is not limitless either.

I keep canisters, which are commonly kept on the counter, inside the cabinets. Even though they are a set, I make no effort to keep them together. I put them in a cabinet nearest the place I usually use them. Don't stick your cooking spoons, spatulas, and forks into a holder on the counter where they stick out like a metallic bouquet. Hang them from a specially designed hanger or keep them in a drawer. I hang my knives from a metallic bar mounted on the side of the cabinet.

If you are short on drawer space, try the instant drawers made by Rubbermaid, available in hardware stores and other places. They fit under the cabinet as well. One of the things I have enjoyed most is the pull-down spice caddy, which also mounts (as if you could not have guessed it) under the cabinet. Finally, don't overlook shelf units that you install inside cabinet doors.

A recovering Messie can start getting so overorganized that she makes another mess. Get things set up in a reasonable way and don't go overboard.

If you have run out of cabinet space, you can have a long, narrow shelf built between the countertop and the upper cabinet to hold many of the things you previously kept on the counter. If your microwave oven takes up valuable counter space, look for a microwave oven cart that will fit the décor of your kitchen. These carts have the additional advantage of having cabinet space below and frequently shelf space above where you can store cookbooks or small appliances. If the microwave cord does not reach the proper outlet, buy a cart that rolls or use a heavy-duty air-conditioner extension cord that indicates it also works for microwaves.

On the countertop you may wish to put one flowerpot with flowers. That's enough. This clear counter space, so easy for you to use and enjoy looking at, will inspire you to do more in the area of kitchen organization.

Be careful of household tips that may cause more work than they save. I could tell you to poke a hole in the center of a shower cap, stick your beaters through it, and use it to cover your mixing bowl when you use it. This eliminates splatters, but you're left with one really messy shower cap to clean. And where would you store such a thing? It is easier to be careful and to wipe up where you splatter.

I could also tell you to put your meat and candy thermometers into plastic eyeglass holders to keep them safe. Or to use plastic coffee lids between hamburger patties when you freeze them so you can pop them apart easily later. I could recommend that you cut small circles out of plastic lids and then cut an X in the center and use them as plastic bag closures. But if you did all these things, you would be back in the saving-and-keeping syndrome, spending your time ruining scissors and your schedule by cutting out little circles. And where would you store them? In another empty eyeglass holder? Eventually you would need a rack to hold all of the eyeglass holders.

The point I am making is that you should avoid the craziness of doing all this extra stuff. A lot of these types of suggestions are useful for some in making the kitchen easier to live in, but a recovering Messie can start getting so overorganized that she makes another mess. Get things set up in a reasonable way and don't go overboard. Often, especially in the kitchen, less is more.

The Refrigerator

There is probably no area in the house where being a Messie shows up as much as in the refrigerator. The Messie's refrigerator is ordinarily full of a variety of things in various kinds of containers and in various states of decomposition. Messies save scraps others throw away. Perhaps a kitten will wander up to the door, and you will need something to feed him. So you save it just in case. The refrigerator is also full because the Messie forgets what she puts in there. No one could remember all those odds and ends.

The successful housekeeper throws away more to begin with than the Messie. If you are a Messie who tends to have a messy refrigerator, try to put less in than you do. To keep track of leftovers, purchase a small magnetic board with a wipe-off pen attached and write on it the name of the leftover and the date you put it in the refrigerator.

I suppose I should tell you to decide which shelves will hold which items (e.g., dairy products on the top shelf, leftovers and cold cuts on the second). This is a good idea, but I have never been able to make it work. I keep forgetting which shelf is for what. In addition, sometimes the containers don't fit where they belong, and I have to put them on an improper shelf. This drives a perfectionistic Messie to distraction.

Using small, uncovered, square basket containers is very helpful for grouping things. Condiments do much better in those little baskets. Without them, the little jars get pushed to the back and are never seen again. When you finally get around to cleaning the refrigerator, you'll find eight jars of pickle relish lined up against the back, interspersed with several half-used jars of mustard. Round up those little rascals in a basket, and they'll stay put so you can find them.

I should also tell you to use square refrigerator containers for storage because they fit together better and waste less space. However, I don't want you to go out and buy loads of square containers so you can get more in the refrigerator. Messies already get too much in there. The answer is to find a balance. Keep as little as possible, but keep it efficiently.

Other areas you will need to consider when getting your house in order are the kids' rooms, bathrooms, and closets. I have already written about some of these in other books, and many others have written helpful books about these and other practical areas of housekeeping.

Assess the Mess

1. What can you do to improve your kitchen?

2. What can you do to get your telephone area under control?

3. Name other areas that need to be organized.

4. Do you plan to look into any of the organizing books listed on the following pages with the intention of following their suggestions for change?

Books

Books by Sandra Felton

The Messies Manual. Grand Rapids: Revell, 2005. This is the flagship book of Messies Anonymous. It is a must for all those for whom organizing is intrinsically difficult and who want to know the how-to steps of getting organized.

When You Live with a Messie. Grand Rapids: Revell, 1994. Designed to bring a sane approach to the maddening problem of living with someone who does not cooperate with your desire for order.

The Messie Motivator. Grand Rapids: Revell, 1986. For those who need more—more motivation, more passion, more help. That is what this book offers.

Neat Mom, Messie Kids. Grand Rapids: Revell, 2002. This is a book for neat and not-so-neat moms. It is a survival book for families with children in the home. It covers the problem of chores and messy rooms. While training the children for successful life as adults, it builds relationships that will strengthen the family immediately and in the long term.

Hope for the Hopeless Messie: Steps of Restoring Sanity to Your Cluttered Life. Salem, VA: Five Smooth Stones Communications, 1999. An in-depth program for internal change of the Messie mind-set. An important contribution for those who want to get off the Messie merry-go-round, not just by cleaning up the house but by changing the things that keep making the house cluttered.

Why Can't I Get Organized?/Whiz Bang Guide. Salem, VA: Five Smooth Stones Communications, 1998. Two combined books include an explanation of how distractibility and attention deficit disorder affect the ability to live in an orderly way. Emphasis on special techniques and "tricks" designed to help disorganized folks live in an organized way.

General

Culp, Stephanie. *How to Get Organized When You Don't Have the Time.* Cincinnati: Writer's Digest Book, 1986. This book deals in a balanced way with two areas of organization: time and space. It has a unique section on organizing the car and one on helping other people get organized. Culp tells a scary story about how bad disorganization can be. It might make some Messies nervous.

Fulton, Alice, and Pauline Hatch. *It's Here . . . Somewhere.* Cincinnati: Writer's Digest Books, 1985. This is a nicely presented book that includes room-by-room decorating tips, including the garage and porch.

Kolberg, Judith. *Conquering Chronic Disorganization.* Decatur, GA: Squall Press, 1999. Many interesting ideas for seeking the elusive goal of order. Worth reading.

McCullough, Bonnie. *Totally Organized the Bonnie McCullough Way.* New York: St. Martin's Press, 1991. This is one of my favorite books. It covers many topics in a practical way and includes a section on organizing and working with children, which is very helpful.

Special Topics

Hemphill, Barbara. *Taming the Paper Tiger at Home.* Washington DC: Kiplinger Books, 1998.

Lively, Lynn. *The Procrastinator's Guide to Success.* New York: McGraw-Hill, 1999.

Morgenstein, Julie. *Time Management from the Inside Out.* New York: Henry Holt and Company, 2000.

Tullier, Michelle. *The Complete Idiot's Guide to Overcoming Procrastination.* Indianapolis: Macmillan, 2000.

You can read these books for free by checking them out of your public library or by finding a quiet corner in your local bookstore. I like to read at least one of them a year. By the way, the books I have written are sometimes found in the religious section of the bookstore because my publisher publishes religious books as well as books on more general topics. Sometimes my books are found in the humor section.

In addition to books, many women's magazines are excellent sources of information on specific household areas. They often have better visual presentations than books because large colored pictures accompany the written material.

By the time you finish this book, there will be several other excellent books you will want to get. You can also order many of the latest books from Messies Anonymous. We try to keep up with books that meet the Messie's needs and make them available through our catalog.

Visit our website at www.messies.com for up-to-date information.

Or write to us:
Messies Anonymous
Dept. MNM
5025 S.W. 114th Avenue
Miami, FL 33165

19

organizing your time

There is no sense beating around the bush when talking about time management. There are three basic things you need to manage your time well.

A Goal

One of the basic tenets of this book is that Messies are frequently foggy about what they really want to do. They are pushed by external forces without zeroing in on what they themselves want. This confusion, I believe, accounts for the fragmentation in the way Messies use their time. Unable to decide what kind of life they want to lead, they cannot take control of their time to create that kind of life. They are somewhat like Alice in her conversation with the Cheshire Cat in Lewis Carroll's *Alice in Wonderland*.

"Would you tell, please, which way I ought to go from here?" asked Alice.

"That depends a good deal on where you want to go," said the Cat.

"I don't much care where," said Alice.

"Then it doesn't matter which way you go," said the Cat.

Like Alice, Messies have not decided where they want to go.

Now is a good time to make that decision. Decide which way you want to go in the following areas. Put your goals in usable form. After you write them, you will know better how to organize your time to get there.

1. Personal Development
2. Husband
3. Children
4. Education
5. Social Life
6. Career
7. Spiritual
8. House
9. Other

Take a moment to go over the list. Put a 1 by those that are most important to you and a 3 by those that are least important. All the rest rate a 2 and are of medium importance.

Ask yourself what would have to happen for you to reach those goals. That's why we must move on to the next step— making plans.

A Plan

You need a plan to help you achieve your goals. If one of your goals is to write a book, part of your plan might be to get up an hour earlier every morning and write while the house is still quiet.

Your plan should include everything you need to do to remove obstacles from your path. If your social goal is to invite a different couple from church to your home every month, your plan should include who is responsible for cleaning which parts of the house, when it will be done, what you will serve, and when you will shop for groceries.

A Record

To record all this information, buy yourself a notebook that includes a place for your goals, plans, to-do and to-buy lists, appointments, and addresses. It should be small enough to fit into your purse so you don't have to carry something extra. It may be self-made from a small notebook bought at the drugstore, or it may be a specially made leather notebook available in office supply stores.

If regularly used, this book will keep you going in the right direction. The fact that it puts information in writing gives it more significance. Poor planning and distractibility are held in check when we see our plans in black and white.

The Messie needs to realize that she may have a fluctuating relationship with her organizational book. The book tends to require linear, step-by-step thinking. Messies don't naturally think that way. They tend to think in ways built on stops, starts, circles, and unpredictable insights. The to-do list helps balance that kind of thinking, but it also causes some tension in the Messie's relationship with the book. The Messie may find that the to-do list floats in and out of importance. When a Messie is doing a creative mental task that does not require step-by-step functioning, the list may take a minor place. When she is doing some kind of mechanical task that requires monitoring and scheduling, such as redecorating some part of the house, the book figures prominently.

Once you have several goals and plans recorded, you can begin to take control of your time. Without goals and plans, time will control itself.

My uncle owned a plantation that used mules for power even though tractors were available. We think of mules as animals that stubbornly stand still when we want them to move. But that was not all they did. They also moved when they were supposed to stand still, and usually in the wrong direction. And woe to anyone who got in an open field with them when they were loose. I'm convinced that all their laziness was an act to put people off guard so they could trample them to death. I still carry in my mind the picture of rough men wrestling with unruly mules. After the men convinced the mules that the people were in control, the mules would settle down and do the work. But each day the men had to go through the same steps. The point is that the people who worked with those mules had to keep them under tight control or they would go their own way and not do any work.

That's the way time is. It has a mind of its own. If we don't control it, it will take off, dragging us behind it. And we'll be flailing our arms and screaming that we don't have enough time to do what needs to be done. Time takes on a life and will of its own if we do not harness it to our plans and get it to accomplish our goals.

To harness time to our plans, we have to unharness it from our faulty ways of thinking. This means letting go of some things to take hold of what is best.

Letting Go of Impulsiveness

Messies don't like to plan ahead. They prefer spontaneity. They like to act on impulse. Some Messies plan meals the day they plan to eat them because they don't know ahead of time what they'll feel like eating.

As I mentioned earlier, Messies work more on the basis of emotion than other people do. They wait to get into the mood to do something. This kind of impulsiveness, though healthy in small doses, cuts the heart out of a time-saving plan. No one expects a Messie to give up all spontaneity, but it's the kind of thing that has value only when used in moderation.

Because Messies are spur-of-the-moment people, they're often thought to have poor memories. But it's not so much that they forget things as that they just don't take the time to think of them. They often waste time making extra trips to the store because they forgot to buy something. What they really neglected to do was make a list before they went the first time. Learning to write things down will help solve this problem and save a bundle of time.

Time has a mind of its own. If we don't control it, it will take off, dragging us behind it.

The Messies Anonymous Super Flipper System is designed to keep household tasks moving forward on a regular schedule. A little done regularly every day is the secret to efficient and effective time use. It takes the emotional aspect out of this area in which impulsiveness causes such havoc. It acts as your memory for when to do what. Information is available from Messies Anonymous.

Letting Go of Helpfulness

Being very altruistic, Messies let time get out of control when they help other people. Frequently, these other people are their own families. After two days off work, your son John has to be back on the job at a local fast-food restaurant by four o'clock. At two he tells you his uniform needs to be washed, dried, and ironed. It is possible, by dropping everything else you had planned to do, to get it done, and that's what John expects you to do.

Mary has a school project due tomorrow. At seven o'clock in the evening she tells you she needs poster board and some Magic Markers. She says she forgot until just now. She expects you to get in the car and go fetch them.

These children have learned from previous experience that their mother, in her kindness, will cooperate with this kind of thoughtless behavior. Don't forget the part the Messie herself plays. She may actually get satisfaction from rescuing people. It makes her feel needed.

Messies who have gotten themselves into this trap should learn this motto:

Lack of preparation on your part does not necessarily constitute an emergency on my part.

This would make a nice sign for the family mentioned above. At least they would be forewarned. The softhearted Messie must learn to stand behind her resolve and not constantly bail the children out of situations they have created.

Solving the problem is more difficult when it's Dad doing the demanding. He has his wife running all kinds of last minute errands that could have been done earlier if he had just thought ahead. As mentioned earlier, Messies do this kind of thing to themselves as well. It's called lack of preparation. They don't think about what they will need for a job until they start it. All this errand running and preparing in spurts severely cuts into time. This confusion could be cut to almost nothing with forethought. But instead, confused thinking leads to chaotic living and thoughtless, confused people. When we learn to refuse to help every desperate procrastinator, we'll be one step closer to curing our need to feel needed.

Letting Go of Perfectionism

Perfectionism is a big time waster. There is nothing wrong with doing things well, but the unrealistic demands Messies put on themselves make it impossible for them to get anything done. "Do it right or not at all" is their motto. But what the Messie means by "doing it right" is quite different from what an average person means. For an average person, cleaning the pantry might mean removing everything, wiping the shelves, throwing away what's old, and putting everything back in with like foods together. The Messie would do all of that and more. She would painstakingly wash every jar, can, and box; she would ponder over whether the Jell-O belonged on the dessert or salad shelf; and she would alphabetize all the fruits, vegetables, spices, and soups. This is not only time-consuming but complicated, because the Messie also likes to keep cans of the same size and brand together, so sometimes her elaborate systems conflict with one another. Messies don't need higher standards for themselves; they need lower ones. Messies need to learn to say "no" and turn their heads when they see perfectionism winking at them from a messy cupboard.

In spite of Messies' tendencies to lose control of their time, many of us have learned that it's possible to get it under control and use it to accomplish our goals. In addition to the things we need to let go of, there are several things we need to take hold of before we can harness time to accomplish our goals.

Taking Hold of Mood Swings

Mood swings affect productivity. For weeks or months a Messie may rely heavily on her to-do list. But one day its usefulness wanes inexplicably, and the Messie drifts into a slower, less organized pattern of life. Good and useful habits go on vacation. Old disorganized ways return. At this time it is important for the Messie to remember several things.

1. **Don't make long-term commitments.** Since I know these swings come, I try not to make long-term commitments that require more constancy than I have. At the moment I am very interested in physical fitness. I enjoy exercising at a fitness center in our area. I realize, however, that I am changeable. No matter how committed I am now, that commitment may change whether I want it to or not. When the time came to sign up for one year or two, I signed up for one because I

know that after a year I may feel differently. If I am still interested, I will sign up for another year. If not, I'll wait for my interest to return and then sign up again. When we know and accept ourselves, we can make more workable decisions.

I admire people who have more control than I do over their interests. I wish I were more that way. But there is nothing wrong with fluctuating personal interests. We are free to change them without worry. Long-range responsibilities are another matter, of course, and we stick with them through thick and thin.

> Done is better than perfect.

2. **Accept the swings.** They are part of a natural pattern, and they have a purpose. Sometimes they signal the beginning of a creative period. Sometimes they are just a rest period so that the Messie can return refreshed to the more organized way of life. Don't be discouraged or feel as though you are failing. The organized pattern will return soon enough, stimulating you to a more productive orderliness.

You may find a swing in your desire to use a certain organizing plan, such as a certain calendar or day planner. This is natural. Switch to some other way of doing things; just don't abandon your resolve to do the job. Later you may want to return to the previous plan. Or not.

3. **Control the swing.** Let some things go if you must, but try to hold on to the basic habits and commitments. The longer a Messie lives in an orderly way, the less these swings to casual living will affect the order and beauty of her life.

Taking Hold of Dignity

Life is changeable in many ways, but one constant must remain. Messies, like others, are people of dignity and worth. Just because we take a different approach to organization does not change that. Do not get down on yourself because you are not as consistent as you would like to be.

In addition to mood swings, there are other cyclical ebbs and flows that we must respect to fulfill our goals. There is the cycle of family life. There are times when women are put under tremendous stress. I am convinced that men, on the whole, never have to deal with the amount or intensity of stress that women deal with, especially during the child-bearing years.

The menstrual cycle, pregnancy, lactation, and menopause are physical stresses peculiar to women. The stress of caring for babies and young children, being the primary caregiver for school-age children, caring for a husband's needs, doing housework, and sometimes balancing a career are psychological and physical stresses that fall specifically on the woman's shoulders.

Hopefully, the husband will help with these tasks, but statistics show that seldom will he do even half of the work that relates to family life, even during times of special stress in the woman's life. There is indication that more husbands are sharing the work load today than previously. Those women who do have husbands who understand and help should be especially grateful. In the years when the children are young, this help can make the difference between peace and chaos.

When a woman has young children, she needs to realize that this is a special cycle in her life. Her chief responsibility lies with them. But she has got to make room in her life for the house as well because she will be under even more stress if she allows the demands of her children to force her into keeping a messy house. There is only one thing harder than trying to keep a neat house in a family with young children: trying to live in a disorganized house with young children.

Having said this, however, it is important to realize that at this time of life, we cannot expect to have as much control over our house or time as when our children are older or gone.

A single mother who works has the greatest stress of all, except, perhaps, for the mother who works and has a husband who not only doesn't help but is twice as messy as the children. And you can't spank him!

If you find that your life is totally out of control, and you suspect that it is your responsibility to your children that has thrown it out of whack, find some friends who have the same family situation as yours but who seem to be paddling smoothly down the stream you are drowning in. Discover some of their techniques and draw strength from the fact that it can be done.

Messies don't need higher standards for themselves; they need lower ones.

Another cycle to be aware of is your own daily time clock. Some of us are morning people. Some are night people. Some are alert in the morning and evening but sluggish in the afternoon. We're all different. Try to use your peak time for hard jobs and decision making. Use your sluggish times to do things that do not require decisions or zip.

For a woman there is also the cycle of her periods. Be kind and demand less of yourself when your hormones are doing funny things to your moods and energy.

Try to find your natural rhythms and live in harmony with them. You may be concerned that you will neglect your responsibilities and blow your time schedule if you don't make yourself keep going in spite of whatever cycle you're in. Don't think this way. Treat yourself in a kind and understanding way, and the well-being you feel will give you back more energy and enthusiasm than you would ever get by gritting your teeth and trudging doggedly forward.

In this same vein, respect your limitations and interests. You are unique. You have a special contribution to make. Let go of the optional responsibilities that are not in keeping with your interests and abilities. If you have to strain to do a certain job, and if you don't like it very much, you probably have no business doing it (if the choice is optional). You may wish to replace it with something more to your liking, or you may wish to leave that time open to relieve strain from other activities.

I Rest My Weary Soul

Even though we can do much to right ourselves and avoid the fever of a confused life, in the end true order and beauty flow only from God, who made them both and said they were good. James encourages us to ask God for wisdom, and he will give it liberally. This does not apply to household hints, of course—God does not whisper to us that if we put our S.O.S. pads in a porous earthenware container, they will not rust. He orders our steps by giving us the wisdom we need to balance our lives rightly.

There are many women who, because of their relationship with him, have made their lives busier and have wearied themselves and their families with outside activity. I don't want to take away from the importance of working in God's vineyard, where there are not enough laborers. But before we do any kind of activity—organizing our houses, streamlining our use of time, doing important activities outside the home, engaging in important family activities, or working in that all-important vineyard—we need to pause and center ourselves. An uncentered wheel may go forward, but it is wobbly and inefficient and breaks down more quickly than one that is centered. The centered wheel moves forward in a seemingly effortless way, making progress in an orderly and efficient manner. George Matheson speaks of this richer, fuller life and its source in his prayer poem:

> O love that wilt not let me go,
> I rest my weary soul in thee;
> I give thee back the life I owe,
> That in thine ocean depths its flow
> May richer, fuller be.

Notice that he speaks of giving back the weary life and receiving in its place the richer, fuller life our souls, minds, and bodies long for.

John Greenleaf Whittier says it another way:

> Take from our souls the strain and stress,
> And let our ordered lives confess
> The beauty of thy peace.

This relationship can only be hinted at here, but from it will flow the order and beauty we seek.

Assess the Mess

1. Goals are imperative for progress. Looking at the list at the beginning of the chapter, list your priorities.

2. What is your plan to accomplish the goals you have? Are you going to use an organizational notebook or follow some other way of keeping yourself going in the right direction?

3. Are you impulsive? If so, how are you going about controlling that?

4. Do you help others to the point where you neglect your own needs? Are you willing to curtail that part of your personality until you meet your own needs?

5. Most Messies are entirely too perfectionistic for their own good. Where do you see perfectionism interfering with your getting your life under control? Are you willing to give up those kinds of thinking?

6. How do mood swings affect you? What can you do about handling them?

7. What other swings need to be addressed as you work to bring order and dignity into your life?

8. What effect does your relationship with God have on your reaching your goals?

20

finding order in beauty

Riding down the expressway to work on an early spring morning in South Florida can be a wonderful experience, as it was this morning. In front of me, to the east, the sun was breaking through the clouds that had gathered. Heated by the warm Gulf Stream they billowed high, catching the rays of the tropical sun as it rose through the clouds. Beside me, on the flat fields bordering the road, white ground fog, like clouds clinging to earth, hovered above the cool fields. It was like driving through a field of ghost bushes.

I knew the experience was but for a moment. The ground fog was no match for the power of the sun. It would soon yield to the warm rays, and everything would be bright and warm again. The moisture of the fog would not actually disappear. It would just be absorbed by the surrounding warmer air.

That is the way it is with Messies. The characteristics that make us Messies don't disappear when we change. We try to manage them, but even when we have done our best, we may still be forgetful, distractible, sentimental, and all of those other things. But those characteristics cease to be noticeable or influential when they are absorbed by a stronger force, the desire for order and beauty.

Messies love to be involved in creating beauty. Many draw or paint. Others write poetry, children's stories, and fiction. Messies sew, work on crafts, braid rugs, and make hand-dipped candles. Some learn cake decorating or flower arranging.

But you would never guess it from looking at their houses. "Unattractive" is a kind way to describe them. If you look closely, however, you see that the house does have attractive spots. But the beauty of these small places has hardly any effect on the house's overall drabness. There are nice details, but the framework of beauty is missing.

Many Messies are puzzled when their houses don't look nicer after they have worked so hard, so they enroll in another craft class or buy another knickknack. Yet somehow the desire for beauty is not satisfied.

Why is beauty so important? Why do our souls yearn for it? What is beauty anyway?

Beauty is that which strikes the senses in a way that brings joy, happiness, or pleasure. On seeing a rainbow, Wordsworth felt joy:

> My heart leaps up when I behold a rainbow in the sky.

About a field of daffodils he wrote:

> And then my heart with pleasure fills and dances with the daffodils.

What joy he described! And what was its source? Beauty. That's what we want from our houses. We want our hearts to leap with joy and dance in the delight of what we have created. We want others to be pulled into our homes with the lure of loveliness.

But Messies' houses don't do that. They repulse people and discourage them from entering. Messie houses are not a source of joy.

God created beauty with our pleasure in mind. When he planted a garden, he created a tree with two characteristics. It was pleasant to the eye and good for food. It was both decorative and practical.

Messies have been told so often to be practical that they begin to think their appreciation for beauty is wrong. This is a costly mistake. We have a deep need for beauty. Without it we cannot be fulfilled, nor can we get the practical aspects of our lives to fall into place.

> Practicality is the greatest enemy of beauty.

Unfortunately the attractive and the practical are frequently at war in the Messie's life, and the practical usually wins.

Practicality is the greatest enemy of beauty. For example, a Messie may find a desk that has a lot of storage space. It is secondhand, too large for the room, too dark, and doesn't match the rest of the room. But the price is good, and it's practical, so the ugly, oversized piece is welcomed by a proud new owner who has only a vague feeling that something is not quite right. Practicality has won.

Since trying to achieve visual beauty can frustrate Messies, they compensate. They tune out the overview of the room and concentrate on small spots. They gaze contentedly at the pot of spring tulips on the living room table, even though the room around them is graceless.

Another way Messies seek beauty in a drab house is by substituting beautiful words and thoughts for visual beauty. They keep piles of books and magazines around them, frequently in their bedrooms and on the bed. They are pleased to have this much intellectual beauty at their fingertips. But this type of beauty, though important, cannot substitute for the beauty that comes only through our eyes.

Beauty is the mystery and charm created whenever pleasure is mixed in the visual world. This mystery flows from the spirit of the person who creates it and in turn nourishes her spirit as well as the spirits of those with whom she shares her creation. This is what we want in our houses—mystery, beauty, pleasure, nourishment. This can be ours. No more make-do utilitarian living quarters. Beauty can flow from our spirits into our homes, bringing joy to all who enter.

But we must first let go of our "practicality above all" mentality. What we bring into our houses must be beautiful as well as practical. George Santayana, in his classic book on beauty, writes, "A neat plain practical house may have a certain pleasantness but lacks the charm and harmony to enrich us."

When we start our search for gracious surroundings, we will feel as though we are walking from the harsh sunlight of a desert into a shaded garden glen. We will experience a sense of balance and coolness. Life will seem more worthwhile and balanced, and we will feel less tension. When beauty comes to our home, we relax and start to see our total surroundings without having to limit our vision to a few pleasant items.

The order that once eluded us is much closer at hand. Messies generally believe that order produces beauty. This is true to some extent. But in the Messie experience, I believe it is more true that beauty produces order.

There is one other surprising result of having a beautiful home. Beauty lifts us out of our tiredness and depression. Many people beat the blues by trying on beautiful clothes or walking in a beautiful outdoor setting. Frequently, Messies tell me they are bogged down by depression. Part of this depression comes from lack of control, but part comes simply from living in a graceless home.

In *Emotional Phases of a Woman's Life*, Jean Lush writes about a woman's need for beauty:

> They somehow recognize the tremendous human need for loveliness. This basic need is often overlooked in our busy lives. We know our basic needs include food, clothing, shelter,

and perhaps companionship but seldom consider beauty a necessary item. . . . Lack of beauty—ugliness—brings grief to the spirit. Shabbiness and disorder drain us. . . . Beauty creates energy. It lifts the spirit.

Messies work with less energy or dissipated energy because they are worn out by the way the house looks. Depression and listlessness can be overcome by bringing the spark of beauty into the house.

Remember the poems at the beginning of the chapter. Notice the energy words that spring from beauty.

> My heart *leaps* up when I behold a rainbow . . .
> My heart . . . *dances* with the daffodils (emphasis added).

When was the last time your house brought this kind of energy to you? Don't laugh. It can. Walking into an orderly and beautiful home at the end of a long, hard day can give you and your family a new surge of energy. The visual pleasure you experience produces a harmony that will enrich you all. Then begins a wonderful upward spiral. As you are enriched, you are able to bring more beauty to your home, which enriches you further—and on it goes.

So go for it! As you look for order and control, look beyond them to beauty. You will be surprised by how much energy it will bring.

Assess the Mess

1. How does your appreciation for beauty affect the orderliness of your life?

   a.

   b.

   c.

   d.

2. List some ideas you have for using the power of beauty to overcome the force of disorderliness.

    a.

    b.

    c.

    d.

afterword

looking forward

This book is not about the house. It is not about organization. It is not about time use. All of those are important, but they are only important as they contribute to the real purpose of this book.

You want to find a way of life that gives you the power that flows from knowing where you are, where your things are, and what is happening in your life. Many Messies live with an unnamed dread of the many unknowns in their lives. Have they forgotten where they put something? An appointment? A child? Will the next moment require they put their hand on something whose location they cannot begin to remember? Because of their random way of thinking and behaving, they can hardly manage to launch a search and rescue effort. Logical approaches don't work for Messies as they do for their more orderly sisters and brothers who lose things.

Will they spend time clipping coupons, shopping sales, and being responsibly frugal and then lose the large refund check they received in the mail? Do they have a high regard for family and yet have trouble getting the children off to school on time with matching socks and signed papers? Are they committed to their marriages, reading books and attending conferences on the topic, but their husbands dread walking into the mess they know is waiting at home?

Life is way too complex to successfully live it in a disorganized way.

These are just a sample of the difficulties Messies live with on a daily basis. Life is way too complex to successfully live it in a disorganized way. Sure, you and I keep going. Being the remarkably resilient people we are, we are able to cope with the constant stress of the chaos that swirls around us. Maybe we even grow used to the stress, and it feels natural. We show courage in the face of repeated organizational crises. We rally prodigious energy to keep going in the face of that dreadful feeling that something is going to jump out and trip us up. We push through the chronic sludge of undone tasks. And sometimes we feel like giving up.

I want more than that for you—and me. There is a life of harmony and peace you may only suspect exists. Using the insights in this book, begin to pick your way through the cause of the problem. Don't stop seeking until you come out on the other side with a feeling of confidence and power that, for the most part, your life is under control and you are, in the fullest sense of the word, Messie no more.

Somewhere, sometime all of us who live the crazy life of stress and disorder have got to come to the point where we open our eyes and say to ourselves, "This way of life is insane. I will not continue to live this way no matter what!"

At the time we have this thought, we realize that we will need to give up a lot of thoughts, feelings, and actions that mean a lot to us.

Do we keep too many "valuable" things? We will have to stop even if we dearly want to continue.

Do we keep family mementos piled around us and love them all? Some people find freedom and comfort in their piles. People who live lives free of the stress of clutter don't live that way. We are going to have to get rid of some of them and properly handle the things we keep.

Do we have many good bargains piled around? They have to go. Our heart aches to think of it, but we must do it anyway.

We feel the fear and do it anyway.

Do we keep flyers and receipts because we feel we will want or need them later? By an act of the will, we need to walk to the trash and put them in immediately, even when doing so makes us feel afraid and uncomfortable.

Have we avoided medical or psychological help and even disregarded medication prescribed simply because we don't want to deal with it? We cannot afford to continue the luxury of this kind of neglect.

How can I call on you to do these things? Because it is only when we are willing to change ourselves at the root that real change will come. You must "behave" your way out of this. The behavior will stir up thoughts and feelings, so you can challenge them.

Doing what you need to do in the face of your own resistance is in itself a significant change. Other changes ripple out from that. Because you change, your house will begin to change—permanently.

You can pull the leaves and flowers off a weed, even cut it off to the ground, but unless you remove the root, you will struggle with that weed again and again.

Group support is often a wonderful help, as long as going to the group does not act as a substitute for actually changing. You are encouraged to attend a local group, as explained later in the book, or to join a group on the Internet at www .messies.com.

Can you change alone? Many can. Out of desperation for a new way of life, they begin acting as if they were a different person. They simply put off the old ways of doing and put on the new ways that they see working for their neighbors and friends who live placidly organized lives. At first it feels uncomfortable, but they continue and sanity arrives with its soothing, and they welcome it. For the most part this is what happened to me.

I began to realize that I was encouraging immature parts of myself when I walked away from a project and left it half done, when I got up from the table and left the dirty dishes and pots, when I took on too many outside activities or hobbies. All because I did what I felt like doing. I avoided boring or repetitive activities. I thought that approach made life vibrant.

A Messie wrote asking how she could do jobs she simply did not want to do. To use a modern slogan, you just do it. How you accomplish that is up to you to figure out. Wanting to has nothing to do with it. Divorce yourself from this concept.

After a while, I woke up to the fact that waiting for the desire to do what needed doing did not work for any adult who wanted to live a meaningful life of dignity and purpose. I had to sacrifice unproductive ways of living to move into the life for which God had put me on the earth. All these unproductive ways of living were "weights that so easily beset us." By an act of the will, I laid them aside, but not all at once. It took a long while to recognize where the problems lay and to make changes. It hurt, but it worked. It led to a life of freedom and the power to do the really important things.

Once I recognized that I was not going to be able to indulge my weaknesses in the way I had, life began to change permanently.

A word of encouragement to those who fear they will lose themselves—their essence—if they change: individuals are very complex. You have many aspects to your personality. You will not be changing who you are. You will simply be shifting away from immature parts of yourself that probably should have been left behind long ago to parts of yourself that have been underused.

There is a wonderful way of life out there waiting for those who are willing to reach out and grasp it.

Assess the Mess

In response to this final chapter, write your reaction to the book. Summarize your goals, plans, hindrances, attitudes, and any other insights you have gleaned from your reading. Emphasize what you think might be the reason(s) you struggle with this problem. Make it as brief or as long as you wish. Include the steps you are going to take in light of these insights.

appendix a

appearance makeover for messies

This is not just a book about housekeeping. It's about being nice to ourselves and learning to appreciate beauty.

When our appreciation for beauty returns to our lives, other things begin to improve as well. It has a spillover effect. (Don't worry; this is one spillover you won't have to clean up.) As we begin to value beauty and see it take shape, we are encouraged to try it in other areas. We feel a sense of pride and joy in what we are. From this new understanding of our own worth and dignity comes the desire to improve our appearance. At least that is what happened to me.

I have always been interested in looking my best, and for the most part I think I've succeeded. On a television show in Cleveland, the hostess commented with surprise, "Why, you don't look like a Messie!" I was afraid to ask what she was expecting. Stringy hair? An ill-fitting suit? Unmatched shoes? Surprisingly, Messies are usually able to maintain their personal appearance very well, but they don't look as good as they could. The hassle of getting clean (and matching) clothes, coordinating jewelry and shoes, and who knows what else together stresses the organizational ability of the hurried Messie.

Let's Talk Basics

Simply getting up, dressing totally, and looking good is probably the very best place for you to begin getting the house in order. This is the first and most basic routine. When you do that regularly, you put yourself in a position to improve the house. A woman who is still in her night clothes and flip-flop house slippers at noon is a woman who is unlikely to make much improvement in her house.

Bad habits, depression, or poor training may be to blame. If you want to improve the house, you have to start with yourself. Start by doing a little at a time. Many call making these incremental changes taking baby steps. Improve a little consistently and you will be surprised at how far you will go.

If you are used to wearing drab, junky house dresses, get some nice-looking outfits to wear around the house. Don't leave the bedroom in the morning until you are fully dressed, your hair is combed, your face is "fixed" (whatever that means for you), and your bed is made.

Once you have got the basics of dress in place, you will want to keep improving. That may mean you will want to improve your appearance using makeup. If this is new to you, the following information may be useful.

Taking Stock of What You've Got

Organizing carries over to makeup. Too much hurry, too many distractions, too little desire, and too little knowledge of how to use makeup keep the improving Messie from using cosmetics to her best advantage.

If you haven't given much thought to this in the past, your first question is "How do I begin?" You have little or no makeup in your drawer, or it is filled with bits and pieces of past glory that are:

(a) too good to throw out
(b) so old it has all dried up or become contaminated
(c) the wrong color because it is out of style or not quite right for your complexion
(d) okay, but you're not sure you want to use it
(e) all of the above

A woman who is still in her night clothes and flip-flop house slippers at noon is a woman who is unlikely to make much improvement in her house.

In my case, it was "all of the above." I was in a muddle. One of my New Year's goals was to improve my appearance. We all tend to imitate the people we are with, and I had had lunch on a regular basis with a tall, dignified woman who always color coordinated her outfits, including her jewelry and makeup. Her example lifted my sights, and I began pumping her for information. I also started asking for advice from professional consultants.

Gathering Information

My first approach to self-improvement was to go to the drugstore and buy a few cosmetics on a hit-or-miss basis. I was shy about asking for help, and drugstore personnel are not generally trained to give it, so I missed about as much as I hit, and I wasted money on products I couldn't use.

When I realized this approach was not working very well, I got a book on improving appearance that had a chapter on makeup. It was very helpful.

This little knowledge gave me the courage to search further. The best thing I did was to go to the beauty counters of department stores and ask about makeup. There I found a world of serious beauty concern. I got down to business myself. They gave me brochures and samples, rubbed their products on my face, neck, and arms, and gave me advice.

On different days, I had my face made up by four different experts. To give helpful advice, an expert must actually see your face to determine your skin type and color. You need to try products to know which are best for you.

The Wonderful World of Cosmetics

Complexion care comes in two parts: skin care and makeup. It is easy to judge how your face looks. It is not easy to judge whether or not a certain skin care program will change how your skin will look in twenty years.

Before we can proceed with makeup, we need to know our skin type. I thought I had oily skin, but the consensus among the makeup artists was that I did not. When I told them my nose became oily, they said almost everybody's does. As it turns out, I have combination skin—oily in the middle and dry on the sides. All agreed about my combination skin, which gave me some confidence that they knew what they were doing. One consultant said the skin on the sides of my face was "parched," which was somewhat alarming. Her line of products was heavy into care for dry skin.

They spoke of facials and products "just as good as a facial" that I could use at home. They spoke of protecting the skin from the sun, computer rays, rays from fluorescent lighting, and glare from car windshields. They spoke of wind damage and pollution protection and of how drugstore makeup might clog the pores. They spoke of honey, almond, and all natural ingredients. One consultant said her product had been judged by the FDA as "the closest thing to cosmetic surgery." They spoke of hypoallergenic products. They spoke of repairing damaged cells. I had heard a report on the unsubstantiated claims of some cosmetic companies about antiaging products, but I guess the beauty consultants had not heard it because they spoke of that too.

While I am sure that many of these products are helpful, there seems to be a lot of illusion in the cosmetic world on both sides of the counter. Women want to dream and believe there is magic in a bottle. If the product they buy makes them feel better about their appearance, then it has been partially successful. I am not saying that misrepresentation is excusable. I am simply saying that we should take some claims as more hope than fact.

One thing we do know for sure is that skin needs moisture. We all need to drink at least eight glasses of water a day. We also need to seal our skin with moisturizer to keep the moisture from evaporating. I used to think moisturizer would make my skin more oily, but moisturizer is nongreasy and keeps the water, not the oil, inside the skin where it belongs. Apply moisturizer after you bathe to seal in the moisture, every evening after removing makeup, and every morning before putting it on. Moisturizer helps your base go on more evenly and protects your pores from makeup and pollutants. Many moisturizers also have a sunscreen that protects against harmful rays, a mortal enemy of healthy skin. Always make sure you use sun protectors with enough SPF to protect your skin from the sun, whether it is mixed in your makeup or alone.

Rose Kennedy carried an old-fashioned habit throughout her many years of life. She always wore a hat with a brim to shield her face from the sun. As it turns out, she was far ahead of her time. Living in Florida where sun damage is a very real threat, not only because it ages the skin but also because it causes skin cancer, we are constantly warned by dermatologists not to expose our skin to the sun. But thousands lie on the beach day after day. Sooner or later, the skin will suffer because of it.

As I was talking to the beauty consultant who told me my skin was parched, she whispered to me, "The secret to having moist, youthful skin is to buy a bottle of mineral water at the store and spray it on your face with a spritz bottle just before you put on your moisturizer." She looked around and leaned closer, gesturing toward the other cosmetic consultants behind their counters. "None of these others will tell you that. But it's true." As a final parting word she said, "You can buy it at most discount stores." Because I had read something similar in two other books, I believed her.

I live in the only tropical area in the United States, South Florida. It is very humid here, and we don't use heat in our houses, so we do not have to worry about lower humidity in the house in the winter. That is not true of most places in the country, however. If you have to heat your house, buy a humidifier, boil water on the stove, put water near the heat source, or do something to replace the moisture in the air. Sleep with a humidifier in your room. You probably know a hundred other things to do. It has been years since I lived in northern Indiana, and I have forgotten most of what I knew about the problem.

Getting the Canvas Ready

Before you put on any makeup, you need to be sure your face is ready for it. The first three steps should be done twice a day, before putting on makeup and after removing it.

Get It Clean

To clean your skin, use one of the many cleaning products available from a department store or drugstore. If you go to the drugstore, read the labels well because each product is for a certain kind of skin. If you are used to a facial cleansing bar (i.e., soap) there are many of these available as well. The cleanser will gather up the pollution, dirt, excess oil, old makeup, and dead skin cells. Put the cleanser on your face with your fingers and circle gently. Rinse well with handfuls of water and pat dry. For the eyes, use a special makeup removal solvent. It is very gentle for the sensitive eye area.

Get It Cleaner Still

After you have cleansed the skin, use a toner to whisk away any soil or cleanser that might remain. These may also be called freshener, astringent, or facial rinse. Each is designed for a certain type of skin, so read the labels. Toners for oily skin have more alcohol than the toners for dry skin.

Keep It Moist

While the skin is still moist from cleansing, apply moisturizer to seal it in. Moisturizer also helps the makeup base go on more smoothly.

One Final Step

Once or twice a week (or whenever you happen to think of it—Messies tend to lose track of time on things like this), give yourself a good facial scrub or mask to clean away deep-down oil and dirt and to remove dead skin cells. Like all cleansing of the face and neck, do it gently. (Do not include the eyes in this or any other cleansing of the face since the eye area is very delicate and needs special treatment.) Use cotton balls or a facial sponge to remove the mask and rinse with water. At this time the skin especially needs an application of moisturizer to protect it. Now your face is refreshed, toned, and ready to glow.

The Tools You Need

Tools is such a masculine word—let's call them "magic wands" instead; makeup is romantic and fun.

1. **Big fat brush.** The first magic wand you will need is a big sable brush for putting on loose powder. It may cost a lot, but it will last forever, and you can leave it to your children when you die. Some people say you can use your husband's old shaving brush. This is true, but I hate to see you using this

make-do attitude so common to frugal Messies. You really do need a makeup brush designed for this purpose.

2. **A really good tweezer.** (Not one you have been using to remove ingrown toenails and have bent so badly that now it only works half the time and then not well.)

3. **Makeup sponges.** You can buy these anywhere. They come in bunches. They are triangular. You use them for putting on makeup, concealer, and so on.

4. **Cotton swabs or cotton balls.** These are used for removing smudges, blending, and removing your mask or eye makeup. Avoid using tissues. They are rougher than cotton balls. You may wish to have some cotton swabs on hand for blending eye makeup.

5. **Makeup mirror.** You need a place with both a good mirror and a good light. If you don't have a mirror located in a well-lit area, buy one that sits on a stand so you can take it to a bright place to work, preferably near a window, where you can take advantage of natural light. If you are half blind, as I seem to be becoming, and you have to take off your glasses to put on makeup, you need a magnifying mirror.

6. **Extras.** You may wish to get an eyelash curler and a mister or atomizer for squirting on the mineral water I mentioned earlier. Some people would say these too are necessities. I will let you be the judge of that.

7. **More stuff.** You will need more brushes and small foam-tipped applicators, but these are frequently included in blush and the eye shadow packages when you buy them. Finally, you will need a pencil sharpener to sharpen your eyebrow pencil, your eyeliner pencil, and your lipliner pencil if you get any of these. The pencil sharpener is sometimes included with the pencils. If one is not included with the pencil you buy, it is available in drugstores.

The Paint Itself

You don't need a lot of makeup to look beautiful, but you do need the right makeup. Don't get rid of your leftover makeup until you know what you really need. However, be mentally prepared to get rid of it if you see that it is not perfect for you. Now is not the time to refuse to throw stuff away because you may find some use for it someday. We are going for perfection here. We want you to be special.

Copy the list of products I mentioned to take with you as you go comparison shopping, which you need to do before laying out a penny. You will need to go to a beauty consultant to find out about your skin type, color, and so on. Department store makeup artists, cosmetic store consultants, or at-home consultants will be very willing to give you all the advice you ask for. Many will schedule an appointment for a makeover. Usually it is without obligation, but ask if there is a minimum purchase required for the makeover. They will advise you about skin care for your skin type. Some will give a facial. They will put on the base they choose for you and tell you what kind of blush and what color eye shadow they advise. You will walk away with a good idea of what each product can do for you. Do not feel obligated to buy from them until you are sure. Tell them, as I did, that you have decided to upgrade your makeup and that you are trying out various lines to find out which is best for you. Tell them you are trying several before deciding. Don't be shy and never let a salesperson pressure you to make a decision. One of the products you try will be just right for you. Wait until you find it before you buy.

There are many promotional giveaways in cosmetic marketing. By keeping your eyes open for ads, you will be able to get some of these additional gifts with your purchases.

Let's look at the makeup basics you are likely to encounter in your adventure.

1. **The foundation or base**—the most important part of the makeup. You should choose the coverage and color that is right for you. If you have clear, beautiful skin, you will need sheer coverage. For a natural look, use the sheerest you can get by with. Use oil-based foundation for dry skin and water-based foundation for oily skin. All fair complexions have either yellow or pink undertones. The base you choose needs to

have the same undertones as your skin and should match the color of your complexion as nearly as possible. To tell if your foundation matches your skin tone, test it by placing a stripe at your jawline. That's where your skin's truest undertones show through. The right shade will almost disappear. If your base doesn't match your natural color as exactly as possible, you will have a line where your makeup stops. You will look made-up in the poorest sense of the word.

Brown or black complexions need special consultation because they may also have blue undertones. There are some excellent product lines and consultants for African American women. Many blush and eye shadow colors work well for both dark and fair complexions, but there are some colors that look great only on dark complexions and are only available in cosmetic lines designed especially for African American women. If you have a swarthy complexion and have been getting products from general cosmetic lines, switch to a line especially for women of color and you may find you have been overlooking a whole array of lovely colors not available elsewhere.

2. **Concealer**—comes in liquid, cream, or stick. Liquid is best.

3. **Powder blushes**—two or three shades are enough.

4. **Loose powder**—translucent or matching foundation.

5. **Eye shadow**—four shades will do; the colors vary with fashion.

6. **Eyeliner pencil**—voted "most valued" makeup tool because of how it highlights the eyes.

7. **Lipliner**—adds fashion and keeps lipstick from "feathering."

8. **Lipstick**—gloss, creamy, stay-on.

9. **Mascara**—special occasions for most, everyday use for many.

There are other cosmetics you may want to get, but we will mention these as we go along. Remember, it is your choice whether they are expensive or inexpensive. Whatever you get may exceed your makeup budget right now, so take it easy and add as you go.

The Beauty Begins

Now that your face is clean and moisturized and you have assembled the products you need, let's go!

1. Put on the makeup base using either your fingers or the makeup sponge. Smooth it evenly over the face, paying special attention to the lines of your jaw, chin, and hair. Blend it evenly and gently. Don't worry if it gets on your lips. That will just help set your lipstick later.

2. Dot the concealer on any blemishes—spidery veins, dark spots, or dark under-eye circles—that show through the base. Don't rub it in. Just touch it on lightly with your finger. Too much concealer or too much rubbing will only exaggerate the imperfection.

3. Cheek color comes next. Locate your cheekbones with your fingers. In a kidney shape, from the cheekbone just below the center of the eye at its widest point and curving just up to the temple at it narrowest point, add powder blush that complements your makeup and the clothes you are wearing. Blend it in gently until it looks as though the glow is part of your own cheek. Dot a gentle touch of color on the tip of the nose and on the chin and blend in till it looks like a natural part of your glow.

Although many blushes come in sets of two with the instructions to contour with the darker color, I don't recommend it as a regular thing. A simple one-color blush seems to look nicest.

Another good hint to remember is to put cream rouge on before the powder blush because the cream lasts longer.

4. Eye color is where a person's own distinctive style stands out and where fashion changes show up first. Teenagers just starting out do strange and wonderful things with eye makeup. They can play with makeup and get away with it. Most women, however, want eye shadow to enhance their eyes while looking natural. Skill and practice are required to do this.

The eyeliner should be put on with a pencil that matches your eye shadow. Some people line the whole eye with the pencil. Many who wish to make their eyes look larger and more natural run the pencil only from the center of the bottom lid to just beyond the outer corner. The more completely you outline your eye, the smaller it tends to look. It is very important to get very close to the lashes, that is, to draw the line just above the lash line on the upper lid and just below the lashes on the bottom. Leave no space between the pencil mark and the lashes.

There are two ways to get a softer look than that achieved by an eyeliner pencil. The first one is to use the point of a sponge applicator dipped into brown or gray eye shadow to outline the eye. Then soften the line with a clean cotton swab. Some women who use eyeliner pencil put an eye shadow powder line over the eyeliner pencil to soften the look. Another way to outline the eyes is by dampening a small pointed eyeliner brush and dipping it into the brown or gray eye shadow powder. Get enough color on the brush to make a thin line just above and below the lash line. This too gives a more subtle look than the eyeliner pencil.

5. Translucent powder sets your makeup. It gives you a finished look and also protects your face from grime and pollution. Translucent powder does not have its own color. It reflects the color you have on, including the blush you have already applied. Don't put it over eye makeup. Put loose translucent powder on with that fat makeup brush I mentioned earlier. Dust off excess powder with cotton balls or a soft powder puff. Don't worry if it gets on your lips. Lipstick will go on over it and stay on better because of it.

6. Don't forget the eyebrows. To make them look their nicest, be sure they are plucked following their natural line, but eliminating any stray hairs. If your brows look spotty, you may wish to fill them in or darken them. For dark brows that need to be filled in, use a sharp pencil the color of your brows. Make short, feathery lines like hairs where there are gaps in the brow. Don't paint a brow on your face. It will look fake. Just fill in as little as necessary to get the best look. Older women may wish to fill gaps in softly with a very lightly dusted sponge ap-

plicator and pale brown shadow instead of the harsher pencil lines to avoid a hard look. Finish by brushing the eyebrows with a brow brush or an extra toothbrush. Do the brows after the powder to remove the excess powder.

7. At last we come to the lips. First line your lips with lipliner. This keeps the color from bleeding or feathering onto your face. It gives a much more finished look. The lipliner does not have to match your lipstick exactly, but it needs to be in the same color family. Blend the line softly with your little finger so it won't look like you have a line around your lips. Now apply lipstick between the lines. Use the lipstick directly from the stick or use a lipstick brush. If you wish, add a spot of gloss to the center of your bottom lip for interest or, as one beauty consultant called it, "that pouty look."

8. You may want to add some finishing touches. I put these touches last because they are optional for me. The first is curling the lashes with a lash curler. The second is putting on mascara. Mascara comes in two forms: mascara that darkens your lashes and mascara that makes your lashes appear fuller and longer as it darkens them. There is also waterproof mascara. For better coverage when you apply mascara, let the first application dry and then add another.

I don't like to use mascara because I find it hard to remove. Excessive rubbing of the sensitive skin around the eyes can cause damage and loss of elasticity (in other words, bags under the eyes).

Now you know just about everything that I, as a novice, found out about makeup. There are lots of extra things, of course, that you will find out as salespeople tell you about their products. Just remember to take things slowly as you begin. If you have not worn much makeup and decide to upgrade your appearance in this area, don't make the change too abruptly. It will startle both you and your friends.

How much makeup should you wear? Wear as much as you need to protect your face and as much as makes you look nice in the context of your life. Makeup will make you look better if properly applied. People will not ask about your makeup. They will say things like, "My, you look so rested. Have you been on vacation?" Or they will say, "You look different. Did you have your hair cut?" Or simply, "You look nice today."

If you seldom get out because you live in an isolated area or if it is not customary to wear much makeup in your area, you still need to care for your skin with cleanser, toner, and masks and to use moisturizer, base, and powder to protect your skin. A little lipstick and blush help to perk up your face. The other things can be saved for special occasions.

The Best Source of Beauty

Makeup is only an enhancer. A life balanced between work and play, regular exercise, well-balanced eating, and avoidance of bad habits will produce a glow from within that makeup cannot provide.

Once when I was in college, I decided not to give any attention to my appearance while I focused on developing my inner self. But I soon learned that looking droopy did not improve my inner self. If anything, a frumpy look is a contradiction to the beautiful spirit one wishes to have. Makeup, like many things in life, has to be a part of a balanced lifestyle. There is a certain harmony in having a beautiful spirit and beautiful face to match.

Deeper still is the beauty of the Spirit that shines through the eyes, the bearing, and the personality. The Bible speaks of the beauty of holiness. This beauty is not caused by a halo and a wispy smile. This beauty is the love and joy that come from knowing the God who is love.

appendix b

support groups

Messies Anonymous encourages support groups to help re-forming Messies keep on track with their goals. There are two possibilities—online and local support groups. Groups with a variety of focuses meet on the Internet on the Messies Anonymous website at www.messies.com. Local groups meet face-to-face in areas where enough people are interested in forming a group.

Getting Started

So you are thinking about starting a group in your area? You feel the need to meet with others and share insights, goals, and successes. There are a variety of ways for groups to start. Sometimes two individuals will meet, realize their mutual interest, and begin to get together for support and fellowship. Occasionally a women's group in a church or other organization will begin a group for those who want to concentrate on organizing. Sometimes an existing group that meets regularly decides to study how to improve their organizing skills, so they include that as a part of their regular meetings.

These kinds of general groups that meet to discuss various aspects of the problem and how to overcome it are wonderful and offer significant help. However, it is not a regular Messies Anonymous group and may not call itself by that name if it is affiliated with any other group or does not use the twelve-step program. This should not be a problem, and in some cases it may be a help to groups who do not want to use the Messies Anonymous name anyway. Organizing a twelve-step Messies Anonymous group will be explained in the next appendix.

For you it may be as simple as asking others in your social or church circle if they would like to form a support group. In this case the group may decide to meet for six weeks, thirteen weeks, or indefinitely.

Sometimes one person will catch a vision of how a group could benefit her personally as well as the community. She will advertise using a local paper or radio station, inviting interested persons to call her. Some groups grow as they advertise and function over a long period of time, incorporating new members as they go. Others continue with the original members until their needs are met and then disband.

The General Support Group

There are many materials to be used at group meetings. The books and videos by Sandra Felton are useful. Other authors who deal with special problems may be helpful as well. The group members may wish to read one book together a little at a time, discuss it, and implement it in their homes. Or the group may discuss a topic and have individuals set goals for their own situations and report on how the house is improving. The possibilities are varied. Usually the focus is how to improve the organization of the house. Sometimes partnerships are started, as in the M.A. ClutterBuddy program. Mentors may be of special help to those who are struggling. Obviously, leadership is important in deciding the agenda for each program.

The Objectives

The group has several objectives. The first is encouragement. If there was one word to describe my life as a Messie, it was *frustrating*. Many women have said with relief, "I thought I was the only one." By the time some Messies get to the first group meeting, they have developed a great deal of confusion and discouragement about the problem and their inability to control it.

The second goal is motivation. The focus on organizing objectives is kept sharp by talking regularly about the past week's successes and goals for the coming week. Those who come to the meeting are encouraged to write down their goals for the coming week. That way they make them more specific, and the commitment is stronger. They are also encouraged to share their successes of the last week with the group. To make sure each person has the opportunity to both tell of past successes and set future goals, members of large support groups will need to break up into smaller groups to make sure they have time. Hearing of others' successes, telling of our own, and setting specific goals act as powerful motivation for the Messie.

The final goal of the support group is to offer information. The group may read an article or part of a book on an appropriate subject. They may each read a paragraph and make comments as they go. They may have one member review a chapter of a book about household organization or cleaning. They may have a member tell the story of how she met the problem and solved it. On some occasions an outsider might speak to the group. After the meeting more informal sharing will take place.

Since this type of group focuses on the house, members may want to share what has helped them. For instance, it is helpful to know about a product that works well for cleaning bathroom fixtures in an area that has hard water.

Finally, some support groups may want to act as community representatives concerning the problem of disorganization. They may contact the lifestyle editor of the local newspaper and volunteer information for articles on the subject of household organization. Three particularly good times of the year to suggest these articles are spring, when people commonly think about housecleaning; fall, when holiday preparation stresses organization in the home; and the beginning of the year, when people are thinking about New Year's resolutions. You will be amazed at the interest in stories of people who have overcome the problem of messiness.

The Members

It is usually women who are involved in groups, though men certainly have their organizational problems, as many women will testify. If the group consists primarily of women, give some thought to what to do with children who come with their mothers to the meeting. If the group meets in a church where nursery facilities are available, the problem can be solved by hiring someone to oversee the children while the group is in session. Each group needs to address its own needs as they come up.

The Organization

There are two kinds of organization: informal and formal. Most groups will be informal because the reason the members are meeting does not require a lot of structure. A few people meet together and voluntarily take roles of leadership. Sometimes leadership is rotated among the members. Decisions are made by the leader or by consensus. There are no dues or official membership. Funds are provided as needed by donations or collections. No official bank account is opened. The funds are small and kept in a cookie jar on somebody's kitchen shelf.

More formal groups are usually larger and have a tighter structure. They may charge dues, have a membership list, produce a newsletter, and so on. They may elect officers and function by voting on questions.

There is overlap in these two styles. Most women have had enough experience in groups to know what kind they are comfortable with or what kind is common in their area.

Communication

In small groups it is easy to keep in touch by phone between meetings. If the group grows larger, a phone chain is useful for relaying information. Remember, however, that the phone distracts us from the work we want to get done. It would be ironic if using the phone for the work of a group interfered with the reason we joined the group to begin with. Use the phone sparingly. Communicate at the meetings.

Some groups may wish to put out a newsletter with articles, poems, announcements, and so on. Again, do this only if it does not interfere with the main purpose of the meeting. If you have to spend too much time putting out the newsletter, the purpose of the group is lost. If you're convinced a newsletter is useful, try preparing it at one of the regular meetings.

For new members, you may wish to have a printed brochure that tells how the group works. If you plan it carefully, you can make this double as a promotional piece for potential members and, with permission, leave several brochures in doctors' offices, on store counters, and so on. This depends on how the group sees itself in terms of outreach to the community.

It is easy to set up communication using email for those members who use computers. This can be a very effective way of continuing the change discussed at meetings and of reminding members of upcoming meetings.

Activities

When a group begins to get into complicated activities, it is going afield of its purpose. Keep focused. With few exceptions, the meetings should not be more than an hour. They should be to the point. The group may wish to begin or close with the Serenity Prayer and develop an agenda that they follow consistently. For example:

Welcome
Group reading of the purpose
Report on successes of the week (in groups of two)
Reading of material or presentation by member
Brief discussion
Serenity Prayer

The group may wish to display books for sale (some may be purchased for group discount from M.A. headquarters) or for lending. If the facilities permit, some refreshments may be served, but they should be minimal (unless, of course, you're meeting at a restaurant). On special occasions the group may want to have a potluck meal. Keep it simple and short. Don't let this group or any other group take time from your primary commitment. Use it for your own good. Don't let it use you. That's what this is all about.

Assess the Mess

1. Would a local support group help you meet your goals?

   ☐ Yes
   ☐ No

2. If so, how can you begin one if there is not one in your area? (Check as many of the following as apply.)

   ☐ A friend can meet with me.
   ☐ I can form a group as a part of an organization I now belong to.
   ☐ I can advertise using a local paper, flyer, or radio station (they frequently carry public service announcements without charge).
   ☐ I can post my intentions to start a group on the local support group page of www.messies.com. I can also look over the past postings there to see if others from my area are interested.
   ☐ Other

3. When would be a convenient time for you to meet?

   ☐ Morning
   ☐ Afternoon
   ☐ Evening
   ☐ Other (e.g., over lunch)

4. Where might you meet once your group is started?

   ☐ A church meeting room
   ☐ A hospital meeting room
   ☐ A restaurant
   ☐ Other

Two can accomplish more than twice as much as one, for the results can be much better. If one falls, the other pulls him up. . . . Three is even better, for a triple-braided cord is not easily broken.

Ecclesiastes 4:9–12 TLB

Books

Order the thirty-six-page booklet *Let's Get it Together, Step by Step* designed for groups to be used with reading from *The Messies Manual* and *The Messies Superguide*. Covers the basics of the Messies Anonymous program.

Available from the Messies Anonymous address in the back of this book and www.messies.com.

appendix c

twelve-step messies anonymous groups

The Twelve-Step Approach

Reading *Organizing for Life* highlights the fact that the basic problem for many of us is not the house, it is us. Education about how to organize the house, manage time, set up routines, and the like works for many. For others, concentration on the house leads to frustrating failure or chronic uphill toiling. That is because, to use a metaphor from a previous chapter, they are picking off the leaves and flowers of the clutter and neglecting the root of the problem, which is found in themselves.

To use another metaphor from a previous book, organizing the house without making a basic change in personality is like trying to drive a car with the emergency brake on. I can tell you from unhappy experience that it is possible to do. However, your progress will be poor. It is inefficient and hard on the car. Eventually, the car will rebel and progress will stop. Changing yourself is like letting off the emergency brake. Once that is done, real and more permanent change occurs with less effort.

Because internal change is necessary with many of us who see ourselves in the chapters of this book, the twelve-step approach focuses on the individual. As we change, the house changes. Over the long haul, there is less backsliding with this approach. Organizing the house using tried and true principles becomes a natural part of our new outlook.

How Twelve-Step Groups Work

Very few people come to a meeting just because they don't have anything better to do. They come because they are hurting. They may be facing a personal crisis that has driven them to seek help. Perhaps a landlord is threatening, the health department has been called in, their family is complaining and has issued an ultimatum, or they have grown sick of the chronic pressure of having to live with the consequences of having so much stuff. Whatever brings them to the meeting, they deserve to find the kind of dynamic help they seek.

Twelve-step programs are all patterned after Alcoholics Anonymous. Generally this includes a prescribed program that differs markedly from other kinds of meeting. The procedure follows a written format that is read by a member of the group. Generally it follows this pattern: Serenity Prayer, welcome, reading of the Twelve Steps and Traditions in their entirety, short inspirational reading, announcements and contributions, program conducted by a member who discusses a topic meaningful to him or her, sharing, closing, and prayer. Placards with M.A. slogans are displayed in the room.

Certain traditions have proved valuable over the five or six decades this kind of program has been used:

Reading the Format

Yes, it is repetitious. That is part of its effectiveness. There is no boss or official leader. The direction given by the Steps and Traditions that are read as part of the format provide direction for the group.

Follow the Plan

Remember that Messies are disorganized people who have a hard time setting and observing limits. For this reason, it is very important that no individual be allowed to disrupt the orderly flow of the meetings, which have been planned ahead of time.

No Crosstalk

For the newcomer this is perhaps the most unusual part of the procedure. However, it is one of the most important. There should never be spontaneous discussion or asking of questions during the program. An individual who does not have a part in the program is offered only one time to speak during the meeting. That is during the sharing time when he or she may participate if desired. After the meeting is over, members can group together and discuss any aspect of the program they wish.

Keep Focus on Self

We are not meeting to give advice or help others during the meeting. Our focus is on making changes in ourselves. To ensure this, those who speak should be sure to use the word "I" in their statements. Something like this: "Thank you for your sharing, Ruth. As you spoke I realized that I . . ." The person sharing expounds on what help they have received or the struggle they are having. Sometimes it may relate directly to what has been said before and sometimes not.

Atmosphere of the Meetings

Although these procedures may seem strange to those who are not used to them, they set the tone for a serious and reflective atmosphere in which real internal change is possible.

Why the Twelve Steps?

Since the twelve-step program is different from what most people are used to, why not just formulate programs using the general meeting format? The reason is that the Twelve Steps focus on changing the person in a way other formats likely will not.

In the Twelve Steps, which are included below, mention of clutter and disorganization is made only in the first step, where the individual admits he or she is powerless over clutter and disorganization and that life in that area has become unmanageable. The second step offers the hope of being restored to sanity. After that, the steps spotlight the changes that the individual needs to make in himself and his own behavior. No mention is made of the house, clutter, time management, or any other aspect of how to organize. The Twelve Steps are usually used by people who have tried other methods and found they did not work for them. More intensive, deeper change is needed.

Further Twelve-Step Information

Further information about using the twelve-step approach is available. To locate Messies Anonymous groups already started in your local area, check out the archives on the Local Support Group at www.messies.com. You will find two kinds of groups there: already existing groups and individuals who wish to start a group. It will be up to you to seek out fellow Messies in your area, whether they have an existing group or are interested in starting a group.

The book *Hope for the Hopeless Messie* is designed for those who wish to follow the Twelve Steps either as individuals or as a group. It explains the Twelve Steps as they apply to the problem of disorganization and gives more information about beginning and conducting a Messies Anonymous twelve-step meeting (available from Messies Anonymous, www.messies .com).

This book is directed to the Messie. Although most Messies can succeed when they approach their problem from a self-help standpoint using the many helps available, as a part of their recovery some seek help from professional organizers or therapists. In addition, sometimes the concerns of society bring a third group, social services, into the picture.

At various times, each of these three groups has sought out Messies Anonymous for assistance with clients. Segments of each of these disciplines have given consideration in various ways to the problem. Even so, much work remains to be done to understand why some of us struggle unsuccessfully with keeping order.

If this book adds to the understanding of the Messie mind-set, then the purpose will have been more than accomplished.

Twelve Steps of Messies Anonymous

1. We admitted we were powerless over clutter and disorganization—that our lives had become unmanageable.
2. We came to believe that a Power greater than ourselves could restore us to sanity.
3. We made a decision to turn our will and our lives over to the care of God as we understood him.
4. We made a searching and fearless moral inventory of ourselves.
5. We admitted to God, to ourselves, and to another human being the exact nature of our wrongs.
6. We were entirely ready to have God remove all these defects of character.

7. We humbly asked him to remove our shortcomings.
8. We made a list of all persons we had harmed, and became willing to make amends to them all.
9. We made direct amends to such people whenever possible, except when to do so would injure them or others.
10. We continued to take personal inventory, and when we were wrong promptly admitted it.
11. We sought through prayer and meditation to improve our conscious contact with God as we understood him, praying only for the knowledge of his will for us and the power to carry that out.
12. Having had a spiritual awakening as the result of these steps, we tried to carry this message to others who suffer from disorganization in their lives, and to practice these principles in all our affairs.

The Twelve Traditions of Messies Anonymous

1. Our common welfare should come first; personal progress depends upon unity.
2. For our group purpose there is but one ultimate authority—a loving Higher Power. Our leaders are but trusted servants; they do not govern.
3. The only requirement for membership in an M.A. group is a desire for freedom from clutter and a disorganized lifestyle. Any such group may call itself a Messies Anonymous group provided that, as a group, they have no other affiliation.
4. Each group should be autonomous except when action taken would be inconsistent with program principles and guidelines, as described in M.A. literature.
5. Each group has but one primary purpose—to help those who desire a sanely organized lifestyle.
6. An M.A. group ought never endorse, finance, or lend the M.A. name to any outside enterprise, lest problems

of money, property, and prestige divert us from our primary purpose.

7. Every M.A. group ought to be self-supporting, declining outside contributions.
8. M.A. should remain forever nonprofessional, but our service centers may employ special workers.
9. M.A. as such ought never be organized; but we may create service boards or committees directly responsible to those they serve.
10. M.A. has no opinion on outside issues; hence the M.A. name ought never be drawn into public controversy.
11. Our public relations policy is based on attraction rather than promotion; we need always maintain personal anonymity at the level of press, television, radio, and films.
12. (Together) Anonymity is the spiritual foundation of all our traditions, ever reminding us to place principles above personalities.

The Twelve Steps and Twelve Traditions are reprinted with permission of Alcoholics Anonymous World Services, Inc. Permission to reprint and adapt the Twelve Steps and Twelve Traditions does not imply affiliation with this program. AA is a program of recovery from alcoholism. Use of the Twelve Steps and Twelve Traditions in connection with activities which are patterned after AA but which address other problems does not imply otherwise.

Organizing Tool

Contact Messies Anonymous for more information about the Messies Anonymous Super Flipper System. The Messies Anonymous Super Flipper is an organizational system that makes organizing household chores easy to set up and maintain. The system includes a complete instruction booklet, an explanatory tape, preprinted fill-in cards, and a snapshot album using flip-up cards.

For more information on how to obtain the Super Flipper or the books suggested and how to join forum groups that meet on the website, visit us at www.messies.com.

Messies Anonymous
Dept. MNM
5025 S.W. 114 Avenue
Miami, FL 33165
(305) 271-8404

Sandra Felton, The Organizer Lady™, is the author of many books on bringing order and beauty to the home, including the bestselling *The Messies Manual*. She is founder and president of Messies Anonymous, a group for those who seek a new and better way of life. Through her encouragement and information, many have found relief and brought organization and harmony to their lives, homes, and family life. For more information, log on to www.messies.com.

Sandra speaks at women's conferences and is a frequent guest on national radio and TV shows. She lives with her husband in Miami, Florida.

organizing magic

40 **days** to a well-ordered home and life

sandra felton
the organizer lady™

ℛ Revell   www.revellbooks.com